Violin Making

Step by Step

by Henry A. Strobel

Second Edition

BOOK FIVE OF THE STROBEL SERIES FOR VIOLIN MAKERS:

The others are

Book One	*Useful Measurements for Violin Makers*
Book Two	*Violin Maker's Notebook*
Book Three	*Health of the Violin, Viola, and Cello*
Book Four	*Art & Method of the Violin Maker*
Book Six	*Cello Making, Step by Step*
Book Seven	*Viola Making, Step by Step*

Henry Strobel, Violin Maker & Publisher
10878 Mill Creek Road
Aumsville, Oregon
97325 USA
http://ourworld.compuserve.com/homepages/Henry_Strobel

Library of Congress Catalog Card Number:
94-92156
ISBN 0-9620673-6-9

First Edition August 1994
Second Edition November 1994
Third Printing of the Second Edition February 1997
Printed in the United States of America

This book is dedicated to violin makers of every place and time.

DEMONSTRATION VIOLIN MADE BY THE AUTHOR WHILE WRITING THIS BOOK

ABOUT THE FRONT COVER

Each book in this series carries a distinctive trademark or "icon" for easy recognition, intended to symbolize the contents of the book. The trees here are a sycamore maple *(Acer pseudo-platanus)* on the left, and a fir spruce *(Picea abies)* on the right. The wood of these trees is wed into a violin with a Stradivari type mold, shown in the center. The front soundboard of the violin is of spruce. Maple makes up the back and the balance. Pen and ink tracings by the author.

PREFACE TO THE FIRST EDITION

This is a simple, short, practical handbook. It outlines the essential steps in making a violin. Six years ago, in the preface to *Useful Measurements for Violin Makers*, I had suggested that there were already enough "how to make a violin" books. I know better now, although I was not eager to begin this book that so many of you suggested. It's even harder to write down these "steps" with inspiration and freshness than it is to make a violin that way. Simplicity and brevity preclude completeness, except in essentials, and every established maker already has his own methods that perhaps differ from those selected for this book.

To keep it simple and short, but still clear and consistent, I have presented primarily *one way* — certainly not the only good way. At least this was my original intent, but as I wrote, I frequently found myself mentioning alternate ways, in brackets and small type, [like this]. The methods given are simple and mostly traditional, but do not necessarily follow any one school to the letter. The outline pattern offered here is simply a good example, taken from a violin that was at hand; use any other that you like.

Although I have made relatively few instruments, I have examined or repaired a multitude, and studied in depth much of the literature of violin making. "*Ars longa, vita brevis.*" There is little new here, but the organization and writing are my own, grounded throughout on my own experience. I include references to my other books in this series, which many readers already have, to avoid duplication of material. This book is basic and reliable, unburdened by conjecture, "secrets", or "science". I did my best, within the limits of my knowledge, expertise, and time. I welcome your suggestions or corrections for future editions. Far better craftsmen than I have been making violins this way for hundreds of years. But most of them didn't write books.

Countless violins, superficially similar, have been made by thousands of makers, whose relative artistry is restricted to a narrow range and then subjectively judged. It is hard to stand out when we are all making essentially the same thing. Violin makers, rather rare fifty years ago, are everywhere today. A school can teach technical competence, perhaps not artistry. A book can insure neither, but it can help some readers avoid obstacles and eccentricity in reinventing this wonderful wheel. Making a mere fiddle is a trivial task, making an artist's instrument is not.

This book does:
  ✓ Provide the beginner *a consistent, convenient outline* of the essential steps.
  ✓ *Organize and review* the process for the experienced but occasional maker.

It does not:
  ✓ Specify details of style and finish that are properly personal to the individual maker.
  ✓ Insure making a beautiful or good sounding violin, which depends on many things.

It assumes that:
  ✓ The maker is a dedicated, disciplined craftsman and a *student* of art, whatever his age.
  ✓ He has the artistic taste, musical sensibility, and interest to *pursue* his art.

Making a fine violin is more than copying, more than following directions. It is the individual completion of an artist's plan. It fills two needs: that of the violinist who wants a special instrument, beautiful in form and function, and that of the maker who is moved to create it.

Henry A. Strobel
Aumsville, Oregon
January 1994

TABLE OF CONTENTS

BEFORE STARTING

First, there are several things to consider.

What are we making? The process outlined here is for making a **modern full size violin.** The set of patterns in this book is only one example. Please use another if you prefer. Most of the procedures also apply to larger and smaller instruments of the violin family, with one or two piece backs, different models, etc. But, as promised, I will follow through with **one particular construction order and set of procedures** in the interest of simplicity and clarity. Actually, I have mentioned numerous alternative procedures. As stated in the PREFACE, these are set off from the main course of the text in brackets and small type, [thus].

*There are **two different sets** of photographs in this book. One set is to **demonstrate** the tools and techniques I am using as I make a violin along with you. Those in the other set are all identified by "Bisiach" in the captions, and show the style and details of the **model** violin from which the full size drawings at the center of the book were taken. Neither my violin nor yours will be really a **copy** of it. See THE MODEL in the next chapter for further explanation.*

About the **writing style** of this book — I have used **boldface** to indicate new subjects, steps, and tools. I used *italics* for emphasis or citation. I'm sure I haven't been completely consistent or successful, but clarity was the objective.

This book has to be a **compromise** for different readers in different situations. Otherwise it would defeat its own purpose and become unmanageably complicated. Highly skilled makers won't need this book, but may want to peruse it on principle. Others are perhaps reading it for help in making their first violin. They will have different needs in tools, fixtures, and materials. The *professional* maker will want his shop equipped with the best, poor equipment being poor economy. The *beginner* may prefer or need to get by with the bare essentials.

TOOLS AND PROCEDURES

Our compromise will be to select a **few, simple, professional quality tools** such as would be found in a typical small shop (like mine). You will have to make your own adaptations as appropriate. We will try to use simple but elegant and efficient (workmanlike) procedures. Any part of the process could of course be accelerated and standardized to any degree by mass production or automation techniques, but I am not writing as a consultant to a fiddle factory.

Keep your tool selection simple, only those best for your purpose, and get to know them well.

I have to assume that you know how to use these tools, and use them safely. This book will not tell how to hold a gouge nor the exact size to use. Special jigs or setups are described without detailed plans. The craftsman will adapt these to his particular tools, materials, and needs. A degree of improvisation and ingenuity is involved in violin making as in other specialized crafts.

Another compromise I had to make was in choosing **particular procedures** to use. I know there are perhaps a dozen different good ways for every step. What you make is more important than how you make it. Indeed it *could* be argued that a book or an instructor is not needed to make a violin, that one need merely examine one to make another. But there is also the accumulated tradition and insight, the experience and evolved methodology of past makers and their intuitive *understanding* of the violin. This book tries to hand on some of this.

Methods also depend on your choice of tools. You don't have to use *any* **power tools**, of course, but for this book I will assume you have at least a **drill press**, a **bandsaw**, and a **sander** with a dust removal attachment. I would not want to operate a violin shop without them. Small, bench mounted models are adequate. And rest assured that our violin will nevertheless be truly *"handmade."* (But if you are a "kitchen table" maker or a hand-powered purist, this book is still for you.)

MEASUREMENTS — These are given in *millimeters*, used by violin makers everywhere. Inches are also stated in a few cases for US materials. A violin maker combines both spontaneity and slavish precision. He learns to carve freely on the one hand, but on the other to account for the thickness of a pencil line, and to scribe "ideal" lines with his knife.

A **table** of the more important violin measurements is given with the **full size drawings** at the center of this book. I have fortunately chosen a very typical violin as our "model"; its measurements agree well with the "standard" ones.

MATERIALS AND EQUIPMENT — Some books start with **lists** of all the things you are likely to need. I considered doing this, or placing a list at the front of each chapter. I think this is intimidating and inflexible, and might lead to accumulating things we don't necessarily need. *What we do need will be clear as we proceed step by step, and, in any case, you should read through this book first before starting.* The **materials** and **tools** are listed where they are used. Only you can decide what you need to get based on your own preferences, the methods you choose, and how thoroughly you want to "tool up." We are not baking a cake here.

SOURCES AND SUPPLIERS — I decided not to name particular **brands** and **suppliers** of **tools** and **materials**. These are naturally somewhat temporary and arbitrary, thus inappropriate in a general manual. Nor did I want to get into the awkward position of endorsing some and excluding others.

Please refer to page 33 of *Useful Measurements for Violin Makers*. Most of the periodicals and organizations mentioned there publish up to date **listings** of suppliers from time to time. Note especially that *Strings* magazine has an annual *Resource Guide* and *The Strad* has an annual *Directory*. Both give international listings of suppliers as well as makers, repairers, dealers, schools, organizations, etc.

OTHER READING

Please note: I will assume that you also have at hand the following **other books** in this series —

Useful Measurements for Violin Makers, Fourth Edition
Violin Maker's Notebook, Second Edition
Art & Method of the Violin Maker, Second Edition

I will **refer** to them both as background reading and to avoid duplicating material in this book. The information in them is a **necessary supplement** to this book. They also contain references to other sources of information. It is my intention to preserve the present page numbering of these in future editions to facilitate cross referencing.

OUR WORK SPACE

We want a *clean, spacious, well lighted and ventilated, temperature controlled workshop*. A window with a view rests our eyes and refreshes our outlook — and **daylight** is essential for judging color. A good radio will be appreciated by most solitary workers.

See *Violin Maker's Notebook*, pages 40-43.

We need to work standing or sitting from time to time, depending on the job. I use a **workbench** 36 in or 915 mm high, and a **stool** 29 in or 735 mm high.

A strong, stable, spacious, *flat* **work surface** is needed. Lacking a traditional solid maple or beech **workbench**, a work bench top could be made from two pieces of 3/4 in or 20 mm cabinet grade plywood glued and screwed together, bolted with a cleat to the wall and with a

sturdy leg assembly fastened to the floor. If a section of this is kept perfectly clean and flat, you will not need the traditional metal or stone **surface plate** on which to set your work up *plane* and *perpendicular*.

You will not find many disorderly types among good violin makers. **Materials and supplies** are sorted and stored in drawers or on shelves. Frequently used **tools** are conveniently arranged on adjacent walls for visible, easy access. Unless you enjoy sharpening, don't throw your precious edged tools together in a drawer; assign each its own protected place. Keep the floor swept of chips and debris. You will appreciate this when you accidentally split off a needed chip and try to find it among all the others on the floor.

In addition to daylight, you will want fluorescent **lighting** over the workbench as well as an adjustable (swing or flex-arm incandescent) lamp with separate switches. You can direct extra light where it is needed with the adjustable lamp. You can also use it, with the overhead lights turned off, to show up arching irregularities with shadows. A built-in **sink** with hot and cold water near the glue pot is hardly a luxury.

ON THE NEXT PAGE — *These are pictures from my workshop. The arrangements shown grew incrementally over the years. They were not planned, and are not recommended as such, but may provide some ideas or information. All you really need is a small workbench to make a violin.*

(I have a small professional violin shop, a family business. Not shown in the photos are the storage, accounting, reference library, and desktop publishing areas, not to mention the sales and display room — which would be more appropriate to a marketing brochure than this technical manual.)

The space to the left of the shop photographs was conveniently filled with two views of the current violin drying in the sun.

WORKSHOP SCENES

PRINCIPLES OF CUTTING TOOLS

We do our sculpture not by *pushing* dull, pliant clay into shape, but by *cutting* away crisp wood with sharp edged tools. I have provided some details below on this essential subject, which is the first thing any prospective violin maker must learn, or relearn.

The sharper our tools are, the easier, faster, safer, and better our work will be.

1—There are *tools with a single cutting edge* such as **knives, chisels, gouges, planes, and scrapers**. These cut or *pare* away the wood a single piece, chip, or shaving at a time. They are the *principal, clean cutting, satisfying tools of the wood carver,* whose first commandment is to keep them sharp.

2—Then there are *tools with an organized array of cutting edges* such as **saws, rasps and files**. These cut or *tear* away the wood in various ways in intermediate sized particles, like sawdust. We might resharpen the individual cutting edges (teeth) on saws, depending on the cost and size.

3—Finally there are *tools with thousands of tiny random "cutting edges" (abrasives)*, such as **sandpaper**. Abrasive wood removal is used when the grain of the wood or control of the cut requires it. Used for smoothing, sandpaper works by a multitude of small *scratches*. Sanding lacks the crisp character of the carver's cut, and produces lots of unpleasant microscopic wood dust. (Wet sanding of varnish contains the dust and prevents clogging the abrasive.)

SHARPENING EDGED TOOLS

This section may seem overlong, but I wanted to give a reasonably thorough introduction to sharpening, which is the cornerstone of the violin maker's skill.

The **outline** of the edge on our tools is usually *straight*, diagonal for the knife, and straight across for the chisel, plane, and gouges too. Some exceptions are those of the round-bottomed plane and curved scrapers.

Note: There is a natural tendency to round the edge of a **gouge** as we sharpen it. But sharpen them *straight across* as a general rule, although for cutting the **channel** the gouge is best made a little *concave* across the end to minimize splintering, and for cutting the **scroll** the gouge is better made a little *convex* with slightly rounded corners to prevent them from digging in.

The edges of all these tools have first a *ground* wide **primary bevel**, then a much smaller, *honed* **secondary bevel** to form the actual cutting edge, which may be further *polished* or *stropped*. (In some cases a single bevel can be used, but in general the two bevel method provides a more durable edge, and greatly speeds up resharpening. The process is also different in the case of the *scraper*, as we shall see below.)

The wide **primary bevel** is *flat* or slightly *hollow* ground, never convex. It is placed as follows:

KNIFE — The diagonal cutting edge may be beveled on both sides or just one (right or left).

CHISEL — The cutting edge is beveled on one side only.

PLANE—Most blades are beveled on the bottom only, but the **block plane** blade is beveled on the top only.

GOUGE — The curved cutting edge of the ordinary **(scroll) gouge** is beveled on the outside side only; the hollowing **(block) gouge** is beveled on the inside only.

The width and **angle** of the bevel depends on the type of tool and the material. A blunter angle lasts longer in hard wood, but does not cut so easily. The primary bevel ranges from about 12 to 25°, depending on the tool and its use. The secondary bevel is very narrow and perhaps just a degree or two more than the primary.

The subject of **sharpening** could readily fill a book; we will give here first some general **principles and procedures** that are valid no matter what particular sharpening equipment you use. Good tool catalogs present a bewildering array of equipment for sharpening. What you use is not so important as perfecting your use of it. Sharpening success depends on developing a feel for it, since the edge we need is too small to see.

Sharpening proceeds through three nominal stages — **grinding, honing,** and **polishing**. The dividing lines are not hard and fast, but material is removed more slowly and smoothly as we proceed through these stages.

1—**Grinding** is forming or renewing the primary bevel, using a relatively coarse, fast cutting abrasive. Grinding is done infrequently, usually only when the tool is made, or has been damaged, or has been rehoned several times.

Hand grinding on a **flat stone** is traditional and satisfactory. An 800 grit synthetic **Japanese waterstone** is suggested. It is advisable to use an **angle guide** for precise control of the bevel angle until you have developed the "feel" for it.

Great care is needed with an ordinary **bench grinder** to prevent overheating and loss of (the tool's) **temper**. If the edge turns blue it must be ground away or rehardened and retempered. Choose a slower grinder (1800 RPM or less), and frequently cool the edge by dipping it into water. A "white," friable aluminum oxide wheel causes less heating; it stays sharp and doesn't glaze.

A **slower wheel running in water**, which keeps the tool clean and cool, is preferable. Several models are available, both vertical — for *hollow* grinding, and horizontal — for *flat* grinding or honing.

The bench **sander** can serve as a very practical rough "grinder." With a good belt, it grinds fast and cool. Use this when you want to remove a lot of metal in a hurry.

Note that we do not usually grind or bevel the back side of the blade, except on knives, although we may have to *hone* it *smooth* to get a good edge.

Ordinary, **outside beveled gouges** are rotated side to side in the hand as they are ground on the stone or wheel.

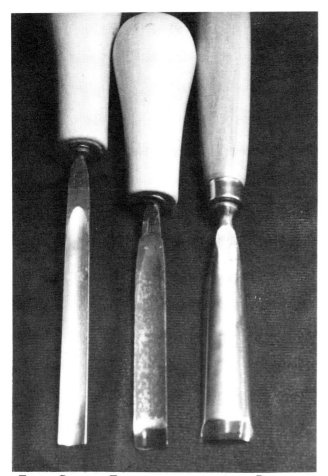

THREE GOUGES. THE MIDDLE ONE IS INSIDE BEVELED.

Inside beveled gouges are ground with a coarse rounded water **slipstone**, a small radius grinding wheel, a coarse sanding drum, or wet sandpaper on a dowel.

2—**Honing** (for our purposes) is smoothing the ground surface and forming the **secondary bevel**, the actual cutting edge, using a medium to fine grit stone. Again, an **angle guide** is recommended. Honing leaves the edge pretty sharp, but with some *"wire edge."* "Honing" usually implies a rigid abrasive, but the word is also applied to the use of resilient, abrasive impregnated **rubber** wheels, or **leather** or **felt** wheels to which an abrasive compound is applied.

When I started in violin making, the recommended honing stones were natural soft white *Arkansas*, followed by hard black Arkansas. More recently the popular choice is synthetic **waterstones**, about 1200 grit, followed with a very fine grit water stone of 6000 or 8000 grit, which leaves an edge so smooth you can probably skip the (next) polishing step. More on these below. Use rounded, tapered water *slipstones* for inside beveled gouges.

3—**Polishing** or **buffing** follows honing. A **felt wheel** is preferable to the softer cotton buff. An fine abrasive compound containing, say, chromium oxide is applied to it. This further sharpens and polishes the edge and removes the rest of the wire edge. It is very fast; use little pressure and great care not to round the edge, which is held just past the *tangent* to the wheel. A laminated **leather wheel** is an excellent alternative to the felt wheel. Or we can do it by hand with fine abrasive compound on a **leather strop** glued to a piece of wood.

In general, the unbeveled side of all these blades is left flat, but we must polish it lightly "on the flat" to insure smoothness and to remove the wire edge. *However*, many violin makers and sculptors do prefer to hone a *very slight* bevel on the back of chisels and gouges. This seems to give better control and of course a sturdier edge. In effect the felt wheel also does this to a small degree.

CAUTION: Be sure that any "soft" wheel (rubber, felt, wood products, leather, buffing, etc.) turns *away* from the tool's edge (unlike the ordinary bench grinder). These wheels can grab a sharp tool and throw it with great force.

FOR EXAMPLE:

The exact **sharpening system** you use is not important; having one that is convenient, quick, and effective is. This is one way. You may have a better.

1—I **hollow grind** the primary bevel on a 6 in (about 150 mm) by 3/4 in (20 mm) "white" wheel at 1800 RPM, frequently checking progress and cooling the tool in water. The tool is held in the hand against the tool rest (except for large plane blades, which are clamped in a precise, adjustable, sliding holder).

2—For **honing**, I improvised a **wheel** of 3/4 in or 20 mm thick high density *particleboard!* It is about 150 mm in diameter *rotating away from the tool edge* at 1800 RPM. The surface of the rotating wheel was first trued with a sanding block or file as if in a lathe. Fine solid "black" emery abrasive compound is applied as needed to the face and sides of the rotating wheel. This wheel quickly forms the secondary bevel, leaving it *smooth* but not *polished*. I use the sides of this wheel for knives. The edge of my wheel is very durable, but it could be easily resurfaced if necessary. For *small* tools this "hone" in fact does much of the grinding as well as the honing in one step. The waxy vehicle of the abrasive compound melts over the edge of the tool and prevents burning.

CAUTION: This method of honing works well for me, but I cannot generally recommend it as safe because of variations in the strength and composition of "particleboard". Weak wheels can fly apart from centrifugal force.

Also note: I use this method of honing for gouges, knives, and *small* planes and chisels. *Larger* chisels and plane blades are honed on medium to fine Japanese **waterstones.** If you have a horizontal, slow, waterstone wheel, so much the better.

[I used to hone larger plane blades and chisels with an angle guide on large (2.5 by 11.5 in) **oilstones** first of "India," and then of hard, black "Arkansas," mainly because I had inherited these nice stones. They are very durable but cut slowly. And the oil is messy and has to be thoroughly cleaned from the blade and the hands. It can get in the wood and cause serious problems in gluing and finishing. Such stones however can be cleaned of oil with solvents and soap, and then used with slightly soapy water instead of oil.]

3—My **routine (re)sharpening** consists in first **rehoning** the secondary bevel, then **polishing** the edge on a medium hard 6 in **felt wheel** loaded with fine "green" (chromium oxide) polishing compound. It takes only a minute, but makes the work of carving so much easier. This felt wheel is just hard enough not to round the edge, as a cotton buff might, but resilient enough to fit the curved edges of gouges.

[A highly satisfactory, perhaps preferable, alternative to the felt wheel is a **laminated leather wheel**, 3.5 in (89 mm) in diameter and 0.75 in (19 mm) thick that is supplied with a stick of "white" polishing compound. It is firmer but still conforms to the curve of a gouge.]

WATERSTONES

If you want to keep it very *simple, clean*, yet *effective*, get a set of Japanese water stones — about 400 to 800 grit (coarse) for "grinding," 1200 (medium) for honing, and 6000 or 8000 (fine) for polishing.

Wipe the tool clean of residual grit before going on to a finer stone. Water stones cut fast and clean, and the fine grades leave a *polished, finished edge*.

They are left in water for day to day use, but allowed to dry for storage. They are synthetic "stones" of aluminum oxide and silicon carbide fused together with a porous bond so they **wear** fairly rapidly, continually exposing a fresh, unglazed, sharp surface. Try to use the whole surface of the stone, since this wear can cause hollows to develop. The flat surface can be readily **restored** by "wet sanding" on silicon carbide sandpaper on a *flat* surface. The sandpaper should be no coarser than necessary — 220 to 400 grit. (Of course *any* stone can be resurfaced on a larger diamond stone.)

Note: Abrasive grit rating systems differ. For example:

Kind of Stone	American	Japanese
Medium India, Coarse Diamond	240	280
Medium Diamond	320	500
Washita, Coarse Waterstone	350	600
Soft Arkansas, Med. Waterstone	500	1200
Hard White Ark., Fine Diamond	700	2000
Hard Black Arkansas, Ceramic	900	4000
Very Fine Waterstone	1200	8000

But note that these grits are approximate; the water stones especially may contain a range of grits, and the effective grit may become finer during use.

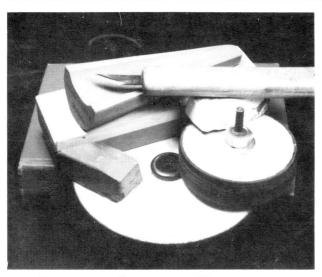

TAPERED AND COMBINATION WATERSTONES,
FELT AND LEATHER WHEELS ON MANDRELS,
POLISHING COMPOUND AND MAKER'S KNIFE

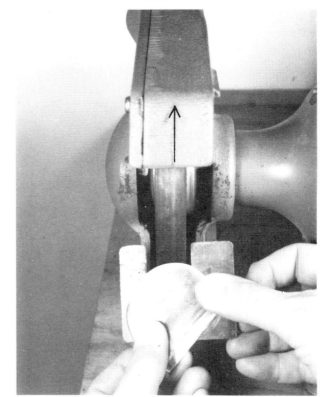

BEVELING A SCRAPER ON MY IMPROVISED HONE

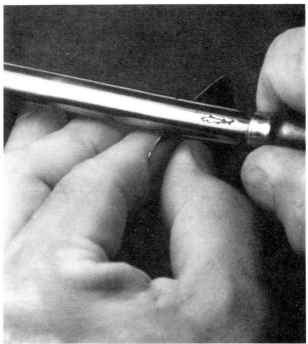

TURNING THE EDGE WITH A BURNISHER

WISE WORDS ON SHARP TOOLS —

1 — Keep a tool sharp longer by not overloading it. Too deep a cut or levering causes its edge to chip — as well as the wood.

2 — When it no longer cuts cleanly and easily, take the time to resharpen it. Both the worker and the work benefit. "Haste makes waste."

3 — A sharp tool is a safer tool.

SCRAPERS

Scrapers are vital to the shaping and final surfacing of the violin. Violin scrapers are thin and flexible compared to regular cabinet scrapers. They are made of medium hard springy steel. Cut them out in various shapes to fit the job. **Thicknesses** of about 0.25 mm and 0.5 mm are convenient. The thinner ones are honed for a bevel of about 45°; then the single edge is turned about 15° further with a **burnisher** (a tool of highly polished round, hard steel). The thicker ones are usually not beveled but ground and honed square, then turned on both sides to form two cutting edges. When the turned edge gets dull, as it all too quickly will, it can be burnished a time or two before honing it again.

THE RIGHT GLUE

"Hide" glue in ground or "pearl" form is dissolved in
water at about 60°C or 140°F. Do not overheat it. Get
the best grade available. It will dissolve quickly and be
very transparent and light colored. It should be heated
in aluminum or glass — never iron, which stains it.

Please note: This is the *only* kind of glue to use in
making a violin. Its physical properties and working
characteristics (speed, strength, control, reversibility,
and easy cleanup) are optimum for violin making. It
also has the property of swelling the wood into a tight
joint, then shrinking to a thin glue line.

We can, after some experience, adjust its **strength** for
the particular purpose, thin (dripping off the brush), or
thick and strong (viscous, slowly running). I use a small
glass jar surrounded by the hot water bath of the
thermostatically controlled **glue pot**. The hot glue will
continually thicken from evaporation, so we stir in hot
water occasionally to compensate, or if thinner glue is
needed. If thicker glue is needed, stir in more glue and
wait for it to dissolve. Thus the hot glue is continuously
freshened and replenished. Turn off the pot when not in
use. If you use it every day the glue will not harden or
spoil; if you don't, or if it spoils, wash it out.

See *Art & Method of the Violin Maker*, pages 58, 68,
Violin Maker's Notebook, page 49, and *Useful
Measurements for Violin Makers*, page 43.

A MODIFIED GLUE POT (NOTE THE SMALL GLASS JAR
AND ALUMINUM WIRE RAISED SUPPORT.)

STRADIVARIUS MODEL VIOLIN BY LEANDRO BISIACH, MILANO, 1925

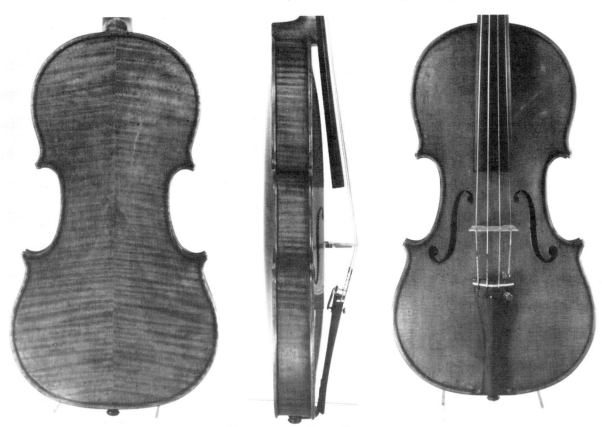

BODY OF THE SAME VIOLIN

THE MODEL

I used the violin that appears in the photographs captioned *"Bisiach"* as a **model** for our patterns. It is beautiful in the classical Italian style (of Stradivari). It was made by Leandro Bisiach, 1864-1946, "the most esteemed Italian maker of the time," and bears his original label, *Leandro Bisiach da Milano, Fece l'Anno 1925*, with his signature and monogram.

I chose to use an authentic, unaltered, violin of unquestioned quality as a model. To use one of my own would provide a lesser or less typical example and might appear self-serving.

Some remarks on its **style**: Everything is in good taste, not overdone. Not "antiqued," a lovely golden brown varnish. The fluting of the lower wings of the sound holes is subtle (almost absent). The edges are very nicely done, the channel is not too deep, nor are the corners excessively thick and square; the arching is gradual. The scroll is not deeply carved, especially at the beginning of the volute. This agrees with the pegbox which does not narrow much towards the top. Also the outer sides of the pegbox are practically parallel, front to back, instead of flaring slightly toward the back. The pro forma neck graft is perfectly executed. (Grafting is a repair procedure, and not covered in this book, nor is there any need for it in a new violin.)

It's **measurements** are quite standard, 356 mm long, the stop and neck 195 and 130 mm, the upper and lower front widths are 165 and 205 mm. The middle (minimum) width is 106 mm (flat) on the back, and 107.5 on the front (110 and 112 over the arching). While most everything else is square and true, the upper blocks splay out a little toward the front so that the width there increases from 147 mm (flat) on the back to 150.5 mm on the front, or 149 to 152.5 over the arching. The sound holes are about 40 mm apart, which I have increased by about a millimeter on the pattern.

It is not unusual in any handmade violin to see small **variations** between the soundholes, the sides of the scroll, the arching and outline right and left, and front and back.

The **weight** of this finished violin with its fingerboard, but without pegs, tailpiece, and chinrest, is only about 350 grams (12.3 oz). Even so, the (replaced) fingerboard is a little heavy on the free end.

THE PATTERNS

Full size drawings and **measurements** are located at the center of this book on pages 39-42.

Please note: We are not making a *"copy"* of this violin, nor is there sufficient information here for that. But you can use its **photographs** to follow its **style, outline, and approximate measurements**. These are somewhat idealized in the **full size drawings**, the **accuracy** of which is *adequate, but not absolute.* They are only *guides*.

Everyone who makes a violin, even from this same pattern, will make it his own. **Styles** differ, as they should. (For example, I personally tend toward more deeply sculpted scrolls and edges, fuller arching, and more tapered pegboxes. On the other hand, our classical "Stradivari" model here has a shallow channel and purfling groove, and a wide open pegbox. My personal purfling ends up with long miters, and I make no attempt to change this.)

Yes, I too am making a violin as I write this book, shuttling between the workbench, camera, and word processor. This is primarily to test the contents and order of the book, and secondarily to provide **illustrations** of some steps in the process, not to serve as a model. Although my violin, like yours, is being made from the patterns in this book, there will be differences, far beyond the obvious ones like the one piece back and one piece lower rib that I am using. (You will see from these illustrations that I am hardly a perfect technician. Regular interruptions from the shop doorbell preclude that. I don't have the time or inclination to worry over every detail.) Minor "slips" of the gouge or purfling knife can happen. Let us not despair, but carefully correct or ingeniously adapt. Otherwise few handmade violins would ever be finished.

Here is **how I made the patterns**; you can use similar methods to make patterns for a different model:

I traced the **outline** onto a piece of cardboard (with a guitar shaped central cutout to accommodate the arching) and redrew this for our **half pattern method**. See the **full size drawings**. It is fairly faithful, but of course does not reflect the variations, chance or otherwise, between right and left and front and back on the original violin. These I interpreted as best I could in finalizing the outline.

I drew the patterns manually, not geometrically or on a computer. But if you compared this outline with the geometric one in *Art & Method of the Violin Maker,* you would find that the upper half agrees fairly closely, while the lower corners are slightly lower and wider here. This is a real world, individual, violin; do not expect it — or my handmade drawings — to conform exactly to any geometric ideal. These details will all vary even more as we create our *handmade* violin.

From this **outline drawing** we will make a master aluminum half pattern, which determines the outline of the mold and, in turn, the outline of the violin.

The **arching guides** were taken from the violin with a plastic contour gauge (with the varnish protected by drafting tape). The guides are just that, an *approximate* basis for your arching. They do not include the edge section, which would interfere with their use. There are some small differences between front and back, so I have given both front and back sets of the five transverse guides, as well as the front and back longitudinal guides. You can make your own set out of rib stock or thin aluminum from the **full size drawings**.

The **soundhole pattern** in the **full size drawing** is from a tracing paper and pencil "rubbing" and is full size, *not flat* but following the arching. I have not opened this violin, but the front is approximately 2.5 mm thick, and 3 mm around the soundholes and post. The **bar** and **graduations** will depend on our own wood and work anyway.

The **scroll and neck profile** pattern was made by first squarely photographing the **head** with a long focal length lens to minimize distortion. (There is doubtless some distortion present, which tends to widen parts nearer the camera and nearer the center.) The negative was placed in a photo enlarger and projected full size onto a piece of paper, where I traced the outline. The **neck** portion was constructed from standard measurements and the help of the profile gauge. The long wraparound pattern for the **back of the scroll** and front of the volute was made from a tracing paper and pencil rubbing.

BEFORE STARTING

Please read *Art & Method* of the Violin Maker, pages 27-33, 43.

The **mold** we are making is an important **tool**, and one we will reuse. *Drill all holes squarely with the drill press, and make all cuts square and smooth.*

LAYING IT OUT

Trace the **half pattern** for the mold onto thin (0.3 mm approx.) **sheet aluminum** by taping the drawing to it and scribing its outline through it with a knife. With a sharp awl mark the hole centers precisely, especially the two for the **centerline guides**. Cut out the half pattern precisely with scissors, knife, and file, taking care not to distort the delicate corner points. Drill and cleanly debur all the holes. See the photo below.

Get a piece of 1/2 in or 12.5 mm thick birch **plywood** (or other suitable stable wood) about 220 mm by 380 mm. Scribe its approximate long centerline.

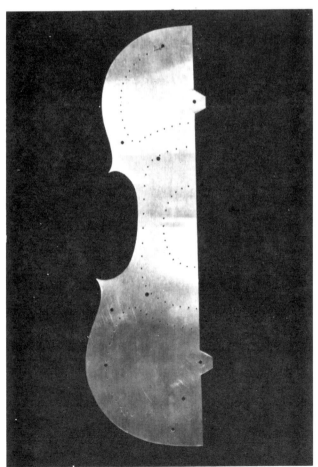

HALF PATTERN WITH BACK GRADUATION GUIDES

Place the half pattern on the plywood with its **guide holes** over the centerline of the plywood. Clamp it in place and drill both guide holes through the pattern and plywood with a 2 or 3 mm bit.

Insert two of these **drill bits** through the guide holes in the pattern and into the plywood.

Scribe precisely around the half pattern with a sharp awl or **knife point**. Also mark the centers of the other holes to be drilled. Remove the pattern, reverse it, replace it over the drill bits, and repeat. Now push the drill bits through to the other face of the plywood and repeat this scribing process there.

CUTTING IT OUT

Remove the guide drill bits. Drill all the other holes as indicated using the drill press. For the **large holes** use a **spade bit**, drilling just deep enough for its center point to show on the other side, then drilling from the other side.

Cut out the mold with a **bandsaw**, using a narrow blade. Stay about 1 mm outside the scribed line but cut right through where the corner blocks will be, resulting in a "guitar shaped" outline.

Precisely bandsaw out the **recesses** for the upper, lower, and corner blocks, cutting right up to the line, smoothly and perfectly square to the saw table. Finish with a file if necessary.

Now **finish** the curved outside of the mold right to the scribed line, perfectly smooth and square. Careful use of a bench **disk sander** (for the convex parts) and of a **sanding drum** in the drill press (for the concave parts) is very efficient. But be sure that the sander fence and drill press table are set *square*, and don't sand through the scribed line!

The mold is now complete except for **sealing** it all over with varnish. Apply at least one more coat to the edges and recesses. When dry, **wax** it, especially the edges, except for the gluing surface in each block recess. This will prevent stray glue from causing problems later in removing the mold.

PREPARING THE BLOCKS

First note the **grain orientation** of the blocks as shown in the **full size drawing**. Select suitable wood. I used Engelmann spruce in this violin. (See *Art & Method of the Violin Maker*, page 38.) Split the rough blocks out to be sure of the grain and plane them to fit the mold recesses as shown. The upper and lower blocks should fit loosely, with about 0.5 mm space on each side. The corner blocks are made *square*, unlike their mold recesses, leaving a wedge shaped space, to facilitate later removing the mold.

Using a miter box (or a power saw) with a length stop, cut the six blocks *squarely* about *1 mm longer* than the following final rib heights, which are going to end up about 32 mm for the lower block, 31.25 mm for the lower corner blocks, 30.75 mm for the upper corner blocks, and 30 mm for the upper block. Accuracy in these cuts will make later finishing of the rib assembly easy; we will need only to sand off about a half a mm from the front and back in the process off leveling the ribs. Check the block height with the **vernier caliper**. (You may want to cut several sets of blocks while the length stop is set for the saw.)

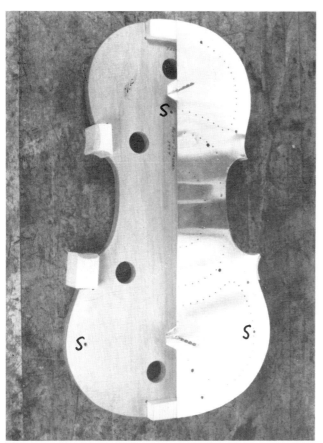

THE BLOCKS GLUED ONTO THE MOLD

GLUING THE BLOCKS

Mark one face of the mold *"FRONT"* and the other *"BACK"*, and lay it, front face up, on your *flat* work surface. Place three **machine screws** in the threaded "spacer" holes of the mold (marked "S" in the photo). Adjust these to raise the mold up from the work surface so the mold is *exactly centered* on the blocks when they are placed loosely in their recesses.

Now glue the blocks in place, putting glue *only* on the one surface of each recess that faces outward. Use about two drops of fairly thick glue, push the block firmly into place, keeping it *flat* on the work surface. Clamps are unnecessary. Let the glue dry undisturbed overnight. (While these are temporary glue joints, make them strong enough to hold until you are ready to finally remove the mold.)

Remove the spacer screws from the mold.

LEVELING THE BLOCKS

The blocks are a little too long, and unfinished on the ends. The best way to level them is with a **sanding board**, which is made by gluing a large sheet of sandpaper to a flat piece of plywood, which is then clamped to the workbench. Grasp the mold and gently sand the blocks on the sanding board, front and back, until they are the correct height and smooth. (Don't make them too short; short ribs will change the sound of the violin). We will use this sanding board again in the next chapter to finish the ribs and linings level with the blocks.

MARKING THE BLOCKS

The blocks were made oversize and project beyond the outline of the mold pattern. We now have to mark and trim them. Temporarily push the two **drill bits** into the **guide holes** in the front face of the mold. Place the **half pattern** over the bits and carefully scribe the outline onto the blocks. Also mark the exact centerline on the upper and lower blocks for future use.

Repeat for the other side of the outline. Now push the drill bits through to the other side and repeat, marking the outline on the back side of the blocks.

SHAPING THE BLOCKS

With a sharp **knife** carve a **bevel** in the excess wood right up to the curved outline on all the blocks. This clearly establishes its location preparatory to paring off the excess.

Shape the (convex) **upper** and **lower blocks** with **chisel**
and small **block plane**. Of course you can do this on
the bench sander if you're in a hurry as in the next
photo.

ONE WAY TO SHAPE THE BLOCKS

Shape the (concave) **corner blocks** with a **gouge** and
half round **file** — but *only* for the middle ribs. Wait to
shape the upper and lower rib surfaces of the corner
blocks until the middle ribs have been glued on.

It's best to use a **hollowing gouge** (with an inside
bevel) and a radius the same as or just slightly less than
that of the block outline. If you are a purist, you can
grind gouges to fit the curves exactly. But you can use
an ordinary outside beveled gouge, too.

[Needless to say, the excess wood can first be removed with
the **bandsaw**. And the **sanding drum** in the drill press can be
used to hollow the corner blocks with great efficiency, but the
artistic maker may understandably not wish to entrust these
"signature" points to it.]

BEFORE STARTING

Please read *Art & Method of the Violin Maker*, pages 36-47, 60 before working on the ribs.

First we have to select our **maple wood**. We could purchase precut rib stock, but we prefer the wood to match the back perfectly and so we will cut it from the same piece. In the construction example for this book I am making a violin with a **one piece back** and the lower ribs in one (long) piece. If you are using a **two piece back**, or have wood only the length of the back, you will have a regular two piece lower rib with a joint at the endbutton. (The maple I am using is from the same tree I used in other recent instruments. It is gorgeously, deeply flamed, and extremely difficult to carve without chipping and to bend without breaking. It is beautiful, and plays from the beginning, but I hope you have more sensible wood if this is your first violin.)

CUTTING OUT THE RIBS

The ribs are cut on the **bandsaw**. Cutting thin wood like this requires special care; the process is called *"resawing"*. A tight, wide blade and a good fence are suggested. The grain is exactly *vertical*, i.e. the annual rings are perpendicular to the flat surface.

The final **thickness** of the ribs is to be 1 mm, so we will first bandsaw them about 2 mm thick, depending on the precision of our sawing.

Ordinarily the ribs are made from three strips, each the length of the back piece they are cut from, about 380 mm long. *(Or if, as I am here, you are using a one piece lower rib, you need one extra long piece.)* Make them all at least 33 mm wide.

One of these three strips will be cut in half for the two upper ribs. The other two will each be cut into two unequal pieces, for the middle and lower ribs. But don't cut them yet; wait until after they are sanded to thickness below.

THICKNESSING THE RIBS

Traditionally ribs have been **planed** to thickness. The *highly figured* wood we are using is fragile and would have to be planed diagonally, or with toothed blades, and much use of scraper and calipers. We will **sand** them to thickness here, a process that is noisy but easier and better controlled.

A **thickness sander** can readily be improvised using a **sanding drum** in a **drill press** with an improvised fence. A **vacuum hose** under a hole in the table collects the dust. The thickness is set by tapping the fence toward the drum with a mallet, or by using shims.

NOTE: The rib piece must be fed past the sanding drum *against* its rotation. And don't let go of it!

The rib piece is fed past the drum numerous times, alternating it end to end and top to bottom. The sandpaper sleeve is changed from coarse to medium as the saw marks are removed, and to fine as the thickness approaches 1 mm. (The final scraped finish will come later.)

A SIMPLE WAY TO THICKNESS THE RIBS.

SELECTING THE RIBS

Examine the sanded rib pieces for quality and **figure** and decide where to cut them and where they will go on the violin. Mark them with a pencil on the outside face as *UL* for upper left, *UR* upper right, *ML* middle left, *MR* middle right, *LL* lower left, and *LR* for lower right. (The top of the marking goes toward the front of the violin.)

Cut the ribs to length as required on a **bench hook** using a small fine toothed **back saw**. Make them all exactly 33 mm wide, with straight, square edges, using a plane or fine sanding board.

THE BENDING PROCESS

Several models of electrically heated **bending irons** are available. It should be brass or aluminum, with stable, adjustable temperature, and a solid mounting.

[The "iron" shown in the photo is something of an antique and big enough for a double bass. Get a smaller one. Or, if you are making only a few violins, a soldering iron inside a snugly fitting aluminum pipe is adequate. Use an electric light dimming switch with an adequately high watts rating for control.]

The **temperature** is set *experimentally* just below the point that scorches dry ribs. Another indication: a drop of water should "dance" on the iron but not fly off.

Bending ribs accurately and safely takes a little experience. It's easy with plain wood, more difficult with fragile, highly figured wood. You have to go slowly enough for the wood to heat all the way through. A **backing strip** of sheet aluminum about 35 mm wide and 350 mm long supports the wood and holds it against the iron to prevent breaking.

It is not necessary to *soak* the ribs in water. This increases shrinkage, raises the grain more, and exaggerates the corrugated effect on figured wood. Dry bending is adequate for plain wood and gentle curves, but I will wet the wood I am using here just before bending. Water helps conduct the heat through the wood.

THE MIDDLE RIBS

These are the hardest to bend and clamp, but we have to do them first. Cut them to a **preliminary length** of 140 mm each. Bend them accurately, especially the end curves that fit the corner blocks. Hold the bent rib in place and mark the ends about 5 mm outside the points

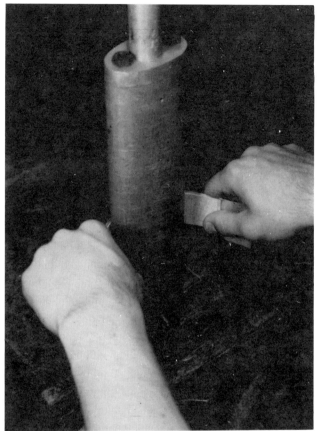

A BENDING IRON (ALUMINUM)

ONE WAY TO CLAMP THE MIDDLE RIBS

ANOTHER WAY

of the corner blocks. Cut both ends off *square* at the marks. Glue and clamp in place, each end extending equally past the points.

There are several common methods of **clamping** the *middle* ribs. This self explanatory photo shows one way. The **curved clamping block** is bandsawed from soft wood about 33 mm thick. (You can saw shallow slots or steps in it to steady the rib ends if you like.) Ordinary 2 in or 50 mm **C-clamps** are used. Adjust their position and tightness so the ribs fit square and snug to the blocks and mold.

NOTE: When gluing any rib, visually ensure that it is *centered on the blocks*, the excess width extending equally front and back.

[The next self explanatory photo shows **another way**, a modern adaptation of Stradivari's use of **shaped clamping blocks**, which can be made in the same way as the upper clamping blocks. (See below.) **Spring clamps** are used here — instead of wrapping strings around dowels placed through holes in the mold. (The mold on the front cover shows the location of these holes after Stradivari.) Make sure the middle of the rib is tight against the form, since there is a natural tendency for it to pull away. The ends of the ribs can be tapped in lightly with a small mallet to insure this.

I realize I have broken my promise to show only one way to clamp the middle ribs, but I could have shown half a dozen.]

After the glue has dried, remove the clamps and complete the **shaping** of the corner blocks for the upper and lower ribs, including the ends of the middle ribs. The curve of the corner block is continued out as the rib is trimmed to a hollowed sharp, straight edge with the **gouge**. (There is little to say against the use of the sanding drum here too, if one is very careful.)

See page 46 in *Art & Method of the Violin Maker*.

THE UPPER RIBS

First make the **shaped clamping blocks** marked *UB* and *UC* in the **full size drawing**. Mark the curves from the aluminum half pattern and bandsaw these blocks from softwood about 33 mm thick. Line them with **cork** or **leather** about 1 to 2 mm thick. (Of course these will be used together with the 50 mm C-clamps placed in the appropriate holes in the mold.)

Cut the upper ribs to a **preliminary length** of 180 mm each. Carefully bend the corner block end first, then the rest. The rib is first clamped *dry* to the corner block to test for fit and length, using its shaped clamping block. It should extend 1 mm past the sharp edge of the middle rib and should make a tight, undistorted joint with it. The other end should be cut just short of the

center line of the upper block. This end is not critical; it will be cut away with the neck mortise. Now glue and clamp the rib in place. Repeat for the other side.

THE LOWER RIBS

First make the **shaped clamping blocks** marked *LB* and *LC* in the **full size drawing**, just as we did before for the upper ribs.

Cut the lower ribs to a **preliminary length** of 230 mm each. (Or 440 mm for a one piece lower rib.) Bend and then clamp them to the corner blocks, but leave the lower ends *unglued and overlapping* where the bottom joint will be. (For a one piece lower rib there is of course no bottom joint, but the bends for the corner blocks must be carefully placed.)

The concern here is to get a good, tight joining of the lower ribs. We want to avoid the common error of letting them slide apart as we tighten the clamps on the shaped lower clamping block. Clamp the overlapping ends at *both sides* of the lower block, using wood pads. Now clamp the mold, lower block up, in the **bench vise**, using spacing blocks about 20 mm thick, front and back, to keep the ribs clear of the vise.

Cut through both overlapping ribs with a very fine toothed **back saw** on the centerline. Or make several superimposed scoring cuts with a *sharp, thin* knife. The first cut is made using a **square** as a straightedge guide. Refine these cut ends only if necessary with a file, etc. to make a perfect butt joint, with the other ends loosely clamped at the corner blocks.

Temporarily place a 2 mm thick **spacer** between the rib ends and the lower block. Push the ribs together to close the joint tightly, and clamp them securely each side of the lower block. *(The "dotted" clamping holes on page 41 can be used for this; I didn't drill these because I used a one piece rib.)* Apply glue to the lower block and rib joint with a thin **spatula**. Remove the spacer and clamp the ribs to the lower block with waxed paper between the joint and the **shaped clamping block**, thus forcing the joint tighter together.

After this glue has dried the other ends are glued and clamped to the corner blocks with the **shaped corner clamping block(s)**.

TAPERING THE RIBS

The ribs still have a constant width of 33 mm and project past the blocks front and back about 0.5 mm at the lower block, and about 1.5 mm at the upper block. We will now reduce the ribs to within 0.5 mm of all the blocks. Grasp the **mold** and lightly and cautiously rub it on the **sanding board**, frequently turning it over to check the progress. Keep it *flat* on the sanding board, applying more pressure where the ribs are higher. *Do not sand into the blocks.* Do this on front and back.

[This work is traditionally done with a **block plane**, but the sanding board is less likely to chip highly figured wood. It is faster and more accurate.]

CUTTING THE LININGS

Prepare the **linings** of spruce or other suitable wood. (I used Port Orford cedar in this violin because it smells so good.) Square up a piece and plane a vertically grained side smooth. Set up a fence on the bandsaw and saw off a slice a little over 2 mm thick. Replane the side of the block and saw off another, etc. These can then be sawed (or sliced with a knife and straightedge into strips 8 mm wide.)

The sawed surfaces are easily cleaned up with a small block plane. The resulting strips will be about 7 mm by 2 mm. We will need 4 each of the approximate lengths: 120 mm, 150 mm, and 180 mm.

THE INSTALLED LININGS
(NOTE THAT THE CORNERS ARE STILL TOO LONG.)

INSTALLING THE LININGS

Bend them dry and accurately to avoid distorting the ribs. Let them project just slightly above the blocks.

The linings are glued as they are bent, and held in place with as many **spring clothes pins** as will fit.

The *middle* linings are let into the corner blocks 7 mm. Make two parallel 45° cuts with a small **back saw** and clean out the recess with a small **chisel** like that used for the purfling groove. See page 50.

[Exactly how the linings are mortised is not important, as long as they are well fitted. Two simple knife cuts, one vertical for the outside of the lining, and one slanted for the inside can form the mortise if the ends of the lining are pre-tapered. In fact mortising of the linings into the corner blocks is not *necessary*, and I would not be doing it here, except that I am demonstrating this method. Note too that, in the procedure described here, we will be removing the ribs from the mold after both sets of linings have been glued in. The reinforcement provided by the inlet linings will be appreciated in this case.]

Remove any **excess glue** from the ribs before it sets.

After the glue has dried for all the linings, use the **sanding board again** to finally level the linings and ribs *flat* and *flush* with the blocks. (Since the linings had projected a little, they will now finish from 6 to 7 mm in height.) This goes very fast, so check frequently, keeping the rib assembly even with the board but applying more pressure to the high spots. *Do not sand into the blocks.*

FINISHING THE RIBS OUTSIDE

Sand all around with 400 grit **sandpaper** on a **sanding block,** or on a large **dowel** near the corners and on the middle ribs, *with the grain*, correcting any small irregularities in the curves. Do not round any rib edges (of course), but some convexity in the rib surface is fine.

Leave the final trimming of the rib corners and the cleanup scraping until later. Set the rib assembly aside for now and go on to make the back.

BEFORE STARTING

Please read *Art & Method of the Violin Maker*, pages 36-42, and 48-63.

THE BACK WOOD

We have in effect already selected the wood for the back, when we chose the maple for the ribs in the last chapter. If you are making a **two piece back**, cut it on the bandsaw for joining. (Otherwise, as I am doing here, you will have a quarter sawn piece large enough for the **whole back**, including the button, and with a handsome figure.)

JOINING THE BACK

With a 14 in or 356 mm **jack plane**, make the side(s) of the back that will face inside the violin *flat*. (Check that they do not rock on your flat work surface. Also test diagonally with a steel rule.)

Clamp the flat faces together in the **bench vise**, wide edges up. **Plane** the wide edges *together, square* to the flat faces. This cut must be very flat to get a tight joint. When you hold the "joint" together in front of a light no openings should be seen. This takes a skill that you will not learn from a book; it works for me, but not usually the first time. One might get a better joint with a long **jointer plane** and an improvised **"shooting board"** (a right angle guide for the side of the plane) to keep the cut square. Take a light cut off each piece.

[Obviously you can use a power jointer for these operations if you are so inclined and so equipped, but watch your fingers! A perfect result is not automatic, however, and the surface may be inferior to that left by a good plane. It's good to follow the jointer with a *very light* cut of the plane.]

For gluing the joint, many clamping arrangements are used, but here, assuming we will have a good fit, we will use the simple, traditional **"rubbed joint."** Hot **hide glue** is prepared, not too thick. Place one of the pieces in the **bench vise**, joining side up. Evenly **warm** both joining edges to keep the glue from gelling too fast. (A hot air gun or "hair drier" is convenient.)

Quickly brush plenty of glue on one joining edge. Press them tightly together while rubbing the top piece a little to one side and then back to squeeze out excess glue. Now let go and this marvelous glue will proceed to make its own "clamp." As it dries it will shrink and actually pull the joint tighter.

[You may prefer to clamp the joint — especially if you use the wrong glue — but clamps should not be used to compress ill fitting surfaces together, nor should they be so tight as to

PLANING THE (ONE PIECE) BACK

THE RUBBED JOINT (OF THE FRONT) DRYING

squeeze out all the glue. Place your adjustable pipe or bar clamps alternately on both the front and back sides to keep the joint from springing open.]

Let the joint dry overnight. Check the *inside* back surface; **plane** it *flat* and smooth if it is not. (Temporary leveling spacers glued to the tapered outside surface will make this, as well as bandsawing the outline below, easier.)

Now plane down the central ridge on the *outside of the back* for a **thickness** of 16 mm, just a little over the final maximum arching height. The rotary plane in the drill press is convenient, but test the setting on scrap wood first, of course. See the photo below.

TRACING THE BACK OUTLINE

For a two piece back the **joint** serves as a **centerline**. A centerline has to be drawn on the one piece back.

Place the back of the rib assembly, which is still on the mold, onto the back, both centerlines exactly aligned. Clamp it there with **C-clamps** on the upper and lower blocks.

Alignment pins through the back into the upper and lower blocks are not required, but are traditional and recommended to help align the back while gluing it on later. (The C-clamps may have to be moved a little off the centerline for this.) Drill 1 mm holes for these alignment pins now through the back and about 7 mm into the blocks. They can be just inside the (future) purfling, about 7 mm in from the edge on alternate sides of the joint, or on the centerline of a one piece back. Makers like Stradivari (and Bisiach in the photo

A ROTARY PLANE

on page 61) purfled after the back was glued on, and cut away about half the pin under the purfling. With our practice of purfling the back separately, we prefer to keep these pins clear of the purfling groove. Now select two small finishing nails (brads or panel pins) just over a mm in diameter and insert them snugly through the back and into the blocks, but leave the heads protruding for easy removal. Now **trace** the outline on the back 3 mm outside the ribs using a small **washer** as a gauge and a sharp, hard pencil or scriber. The **corners** will trace "round," but we will correct that soon.

TEMPORARY METAL ALIGNMENT PIN

[If you want to get the back *precisely* into this same position later when gluing, you could even scribe lightly around the ribs on the back with a knife, but this is unnecessary and might leave visible marks.]

Pull out the alignment pins and remove the clamps. Add the **back button** to the outline in pencil; keep it *oversize* until after the neck is installed.

Copy a **pattern** from the **full size drawing** of the corners and sound holes in thin, clear mylar or celluloid. Use this now to finish the **corner outlines** on the back. We can now compare the corner outline with the ends of the ribs and hope they are compatible. But wait until the front outline is drawn (in the next chapter) before finally trimming the corners of the ribs.

CUTTING OUT THE BACK

Cut out the back, keeping 1 or 2 mm outside the outline. The **bandsaw** with a 3 mm wide blade is best. (The temporary leveling spacers glued to the back will help here too.) Don't cut off the **button!**

With a **gauge** mark the preliminary edge thickness all around at the rough edge at 6 mm. Now use the gauge to mark about 10 mm in from the edge on the *outside* surface of the back, except in the area of the middle ribs, where the mark should be only about 7 mm in. The first step in the preliminary arching is to establish a 6 mm thick level "shoulder" around the back.

You can do this with gouge and plane in the **cradle**, as part of the rough arching operation described below, but, unless you object to power tools, I recommend using a **rotary planer** in the drill press as follows. A **wood dowel** about 12 mm in diameter set into the drill press table, and standing 5 mm high, makes an efficient guide pin to prevent going too far in. Several shallow cuts of increasing depth are used. This is a more precise, controlled operation than gouging and planing, so you can go right down to a thickness of 5 mm. (Bear in mind that the final thickness will be 4 mm, and 4.5 at the corners, middle ribs, and back button.) You can now remove the dowel and cautiously "plane" across the corners, resulting in a "guitar" shape. Hold the back securely and don't go too far in!

[The drill press guide pin procedure just described can obviously be adapted to other operations, including "contour" arching, and, with router bits, to cutting the channel and purfling grooves. We will use here only the traditional edged hand tools for these operations.]

THE CRADLE

Before arching and hollowing the back, let's pause and make a **cradle** to hold the back (and later the front) while working on it. This is made of 3/4 in or 20 mm birch plywood. The photograph will be self explanatory. The guitar shaped cutout is about the size of the mold without the corners, and provides clearance for the arching while the inside of the back is being hollowed. The **bench vise** holds the cradle securely at a convenient height and rotation. Four pieces of soft wood 3 to 4 mm thick, smoothly curved like the body outline, are glued on to hold the back (and later the front) in position.

PRELIMINARY ARCHING

We will use the traditional **arching guides**, one longitudinal (lengthwise) and five transverse (across), as shown in the **full size drawing**. "Half" transverse guides are used here. Their accuracy depends on first establishing the longitudinal arch, but then you can work on one side at a time. Make these guides of thin aluminum or rib stock as you did the mold half pattern.

[You could also use the *contour* system to check on the evenness of arching, or for machine routing of rough arching. Sacconi describes both methods in *The "Secrets" of Stradivari*.]

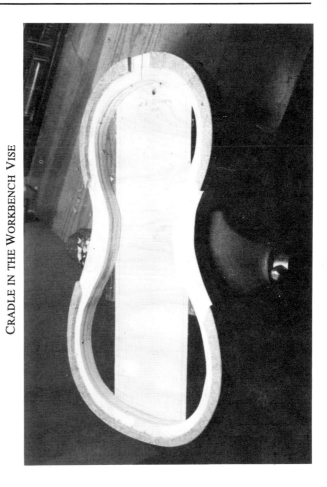

CRADLE IN THE WORKBENCH VISE

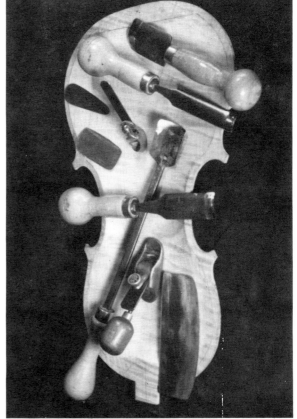

TOOLS USED IN ARCHING AND HOLLOWING THE BACK

Note: We normally **gouge and plane** *across* the grain on highly figured wood to prevent chipping or tearing out. (Toothed planes and scrapers can be used in any direction.) On plain maple or spruce we can cut *across* and *with* the grain, but not *against* it. This is a matter of experience and quickly learned. We have to frequently change direction when working in the middle arching, and especially in the **channel**, where the grain direction is *different* between the inside and outside.

We first work along the centerline to fit the **longitudinal arching guide** (no. 6) using gouge and plane. This will result in a *preliminary* arching, slightly too high, since the channel has not yet been cut. Next we use the gouge to fit the five **transverse arching guides** (nos. 1-5), working *across* the grain, first from one side, then, after rotating the cradle in the vise, from the other side.

If this is your first violin, and if you are using "difficult, decorative" maple as I am, this step may present the first challenge to your patience, energy, and sharpening skill. It is hard work; not only must you cut across the grain, but you are effectively cutting end grain most of the time because of the deep curl. We have to make a lot of shallow cuts; we cannot slice it away in great scoops like the spruce front in the next chapter. One can see why some of the early makers preferred plain, soft wood. But you need to learn to do it to be a real violin maker. And with reasonable wood, sharp tools, and some experience, unhurried carving can be a real pleasure.

[If you make a lot of instruments, you will want to arrange some mechanical assistance in roughing out excess wood. One possibility is the **"contour" router** method mentioned above.

Another is the reciprocating **"electric gouge,"** which lets you safely and easily carve "freehand." I don't have one, but would want one if I planned to make a lot of fiddles. The heavy duty kind is OK; smaller ones may be noisy and underpowered.

Some types of hand held **"grinders"** are voracious, noisy, and menacing. Of course, if you are "manufacturing" a number of violins of the same model, you will want a **pantograph router** working from a 3-dimensional master pattern.]

Having finished carving along the guide location, we are now left with "islands" of excess wood between the guide locations. These we now remove with gouges and planes, approximating the arching. Be *careful* here not to cut in too far, especially along the middle edges, which would cause a "pinched" or "goat-backed" arching. A "full" arching rising near the edge is preferable.

Note that the arching is still a little rough and about 1.5 mm too high overall. This is because the channel is not yet cut, keeping the arching guides too high. This will be corrected after purfling.

The 5 or 6 mm thick shoulder along the edge is now reduced to *nearly* its **final thickness** of 4.5 mm along the middle, corners, and button, blending into 4 mm elsewhere, using a small flat **"thumb" plane.**

The actual edge and corners of the back are still rough cut from the bandsaw, a little oversize, but we have left it so for protection during the rough arching. Now is the time to finish the edge *accurately, squarely, and smoothly* to the line that we earlier traced around the ribs, and which we hope is still sharp and clear. Use plane and knife, finishing with flat and half round files, or flat and cylindrical sanding blocks. Any irregularities in the edge will be repeated in the purfling, so be thorough and critical.

THE PURFLING

The **purfling** will be *inlaid* in a **groove** cut for it 4 mm from the edge. Both sides of this groove are *marked* with a tool called a **purfling marker or gauge.** They are actually *cut* with a **knife,** one at a time, following the shallow cuts of the marker.

The **channel** is the graceful sinking or hollowing that begins midway between the edge and the purfling (2 mm from the edge) and blends into the main arching. Its greatest depth lies slightly inside the purfling as indicated by the arching guides.

[Many classical makers, as Stradivari, purfled after the body was assembled. Also, we are told that Stradivari purfled *before* cutting the **channel**, with purfling 2.5 mm high and a groove 2.5 mm deep, using a *single* bladed **purfling marker.**

Another way is to purfle *after* preliminary cutting of the channel, especially in the case of deeply channeled edges. Also, ready made purfling typically has a height of just 1.5 to 2 mm, so not much can be cut away before it gets too thin if the channel is cut after purfling. See *Art & Method of the Violin Maker*, page 62.

This is also be done if the preliminary channel was cut by a machine **router.** Then it may be best to use only *one* blade in the purfling marker at a time, marking first the outside cut, then the inside, since their levels vary in the channel. In any case, I do find the single bladed marker, with a somewhat rounded blade, easier to handle.

Of course, if you machine routed the **channel,** you will probably also machine rout the purfling **groove** — except in the corners, which are always done by hand. There is something to be said for machining the groove. It is far faster and considerably less boring. As I get older, I realize I would not want to "purfle my life away," especially in this anarchist

Oregon maple, with the grain running every way but that of the groove.

Two ways of *machining* the groove are used. The more obvious and usual is with a **router bit** or **end mill** running in the drill press, with a guide pin in the table to space the groove evenly from the edge. The other uses a tiny high speed **circular saw** running horizontally. I have used this several times in the past, using a ball bit for preliminary cutting of the channel followed by the saw to cut the groove. It is limited to cutting *shallow, large radius* curves; otherwise it will distort (widen) the groove excessively.

Both methods require two steady hands to hold and move the back or front, and a foot operated linkage (or an assistant!) to lower the cutter into the groove to the specified depth, and lift it clear after the cut.

I am not recommending for or against the use of such apparatus. But if you are making only one violin at a time, the set up time and danger of a high speed mistake are not worth it.

After the glue has dried, any of the purfling that extends above the channel is trimmed flush with the **gouge**, and the channel is completed with gouge and scraper.]

In the procedure chosen for this book, we will purfle the back (and front) separately, before they are glued to the ribs and before cutting the channel, on the flat shoulder, using two blades in the purfling marker.

MARKING THE PURFLING GROOVE — We adjust the *double* bladed purfling marker for both the distance from the edge (4 mm), and the width (usually 1.2 mm) of the purfling, spacing its blades with suitable, preferably metal, shims. Set and shim the blades short and solid so they are less likely to be led astray by the hard annual rings of the spruce (on the front). Some makers prefer to sharpen these blades somewhat wide on the bottom for stability in following the curve, or even rounded for marking in either direction. Here we will use them pointed, as supplied by the European maker, and will only pull, not push the tool.

Make a **test groove** first in scrap wood. You should be able to push the purfling into the groove filled with hot glue. I slide the polished head of a small ball peen **hammer** over the purfling, pushing it down into the groove and forcing out the excess glue at the same time.

Some makers make their own purfling. This is beyond the scope of this book; we will buy **ready made purfling** with a light wood center and flexible black "fiber" outer strips. This is easy to bend dry and the bending iron is used only for the narrow radii bends near the corners.

[Ready made, straight all wood purfling is difficult to bend well. But if you make your own purfling, you can "glue laminate" the three individual layers on a form to the exact required curve. You can choose sheets of whatever type and thickness of material and saw this into strips after removing it from the form.]

Pull the **purfling marker** along the edge of the back, keeping it vertical, its blade parallel to the curving edge of the back (or front), and pressing down just enough to mark lightly.

Don't use the purfling marker closer than about 8 mm from the corners. We use a **knife** to mark the corner purfling points freehand, finishing with the *"bee sting,"* not in the center of the corner but nearer the middle rib.

We obviously cannot use the purfling marker at the **back button**. Leave this area unmarked for the present.

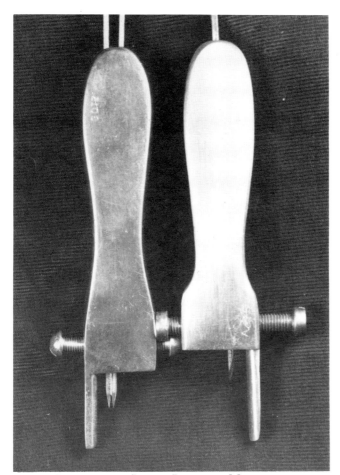

DOUBLE AND SINGLE PURFLING MARKERS

CUTTING THE GROOVE AT A CORNER

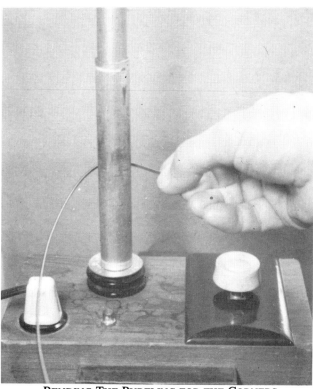

BENDING THE PURFLING FOR THE CORNERS
(NOTE THE ALUMINUM PIPE AND HEAT CONTROL)

CUTTING THE GROOVE — We now *cut* the sides of the groove with a **knife** pulled towards us as the back is held flat on the bench or in the cradle. It takes several repetitive cuts to reach the nominal depth of 2 mm. Be careful on the first cut that the knife is not led astray by the hard "reeds" of the annual rings. You may have to cut down vertically on these first. Some makers prefer to sharpen the knife edge somewhat rounded rather than straight to a point for cutting the purfling groove. This gives a smoother curve and better depth control. You could mark the knife with tape or ink for a depth mark. *Do not cut deeper than necessary*; this weakens the edge. Pull the knife *away from the corners* to prevent breaking them. Make the cuts exactly vertical, and don't go too deep. The thickness of the knife compresses the wood sideways. This will make it easier to insert the purfling, and the hot water in the glue will swell the wood back tightly against the purfling. The bottom of the purfling groove is cut by a special narrow **offset chisel** (or "purfling picker"), about 1 mm wide.

Temporarily lay a piece of purfling in the upper grooves of the back, extending in a smooth curve across the unmarked area neat the back button. Mark along this on both sides with a knife. Complete the purfling groove here.

[You could also mark this arc with a compass of suitable radius, or with a template corresponding to the **full size drawing**.]

CUTTING THE PURFLING — When the groove is complete, **bend, cut and fit** all the purfling in *dry*, beginning with the middle curves. Now is the time to make sure it fits, but not too tightly, before any glue is applied. Absolute perfection is not needed in the miters, but proportion and good workmanship are.

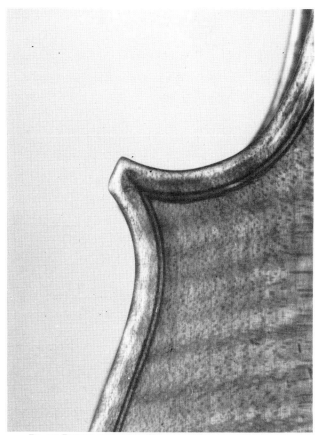

BACK PURFLING AND CORNER DETAIL, BISIACH

These photos show the finished corner purfling. Examine them and visually extend the outside edge of the *upper* or *lower* purfling nearly to the end of the corner. (This would be the line marked by the outside blade of the purfling marker.) Note how the tapered outer black layer of this purfling extends past the *middle* purfling to form the "bee sting." Sometimes it "hooks" even a little more toward the middle ribs, but it never ends exactly in the middle of the corner. Of course the *middle* purfling is shorter, but it ought to blend gracefully into the upper or lower purfling, the inside black layers forming a perfect miter with it.

Since we have **long pieces** of ready made purfling, there is no need to join it in the upper and lower curves of the back. This is no advantage on the front, because the neck and saddle interrupt the purfling. If you do have to join pieces of purfling, a "scarf" joint is preferable to a square butt joint. The *"scarf"* joint is a practically invisible diagonal joint which slants either from top to bottom, or from side to side, of the purfling groove.

GLUING THE PURFLING — Remove and glue the purfling one piece at a time, the middle curves first. Replace the ends first, then the rest of the piece. Slide the **hammer** over each piece toward the miters as it is glued and wipe off the excess glue. When all the purfling is in place, brush **hot water** along all the purfling and wipe off thoroughly. Let the glue dry.

THE FINAL ARCHING

First *lightly* mark the outside limit of the **channel** with a pencil in a marking gauge, 2 mm in from the edge. Place the **back** into the **cradle**, *arched* side up. With an outside beveled 10 mm gouge, first trim off any protruding purfling or glue. Then proceed to cut the channel to the inside of the 2 mm line, about 6 mm wide in the middle curves and about 10 mm wide elsewhere. Do not cut outside the 2 mm limit line. The depth of the channel is gouged about 1 mm deep, and is later scraped to about 1.5 mm deep, leaving a thickness of about 2.5 mm.

[It should go without saying that the experienced maker will probably not mark these guide lines, but simply cut the channel by eye.]

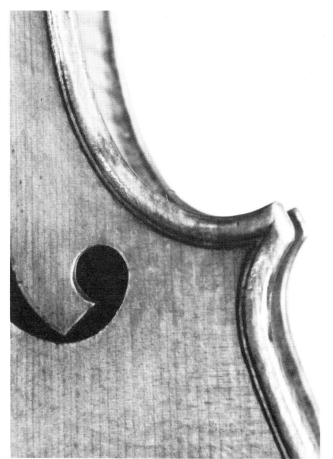

FRONT PURFLING AND CORNER DETAIL, BISIACH

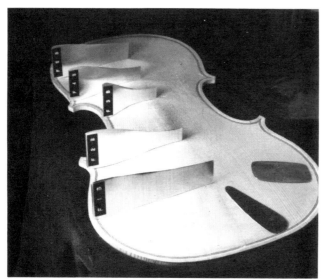

CHECKING WITH THE ARCHING GUIDES
(THE FRONT IS SHOWN HERE)

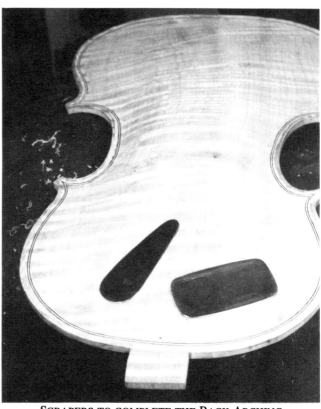

SCRAPERS TO COMPLETE THE BACK ARCHING

Cutting this shallow **channel** requires some skill with the **gouge**, and subsequently the **scraper**. Part of the purfling is cut away in the process. A 10 mm wide gouge with about a number 7 *sweep* is about right for this.

(See CARVING THE VOLUTE on page 55 for a diagram of gouge sweeps.)

This gouge should be sharpened *straight across*, or better yet a little concave in the middle, not rounded. This will let it cut more easily and splinter less. As always, the key to cutting difficult wood is to take a *light* cut with a *sharp* tool.

GOUGING THE CHANNEL

With a good gouge you can cut right down the middle of the channel. But for the refining cuts and scraping you will want to work *with* the grain. (This is especially important later when purfling the spruce front.) First cut the purfling and the wood between it and the 2 mm limit line, taking care to cut with the grain. Then cut the purfling and the wood to the inside of it. Note that the *direction* of the tool has to be reversed to continue to cut with the grain on this side of the channel. Be sure not to cut all the way through the purfling, which would require replacing it.

We now refine the arching to fit the **arching guides** as we did before, starting again with the longitudinal one. The **arching** will be a little *lower* overall this time, as the ends of the arching guides now drop into the channel. The **channel** is smoothly blended into the central arching, and the whole surface is smoothed with **planes** and **scrapers**. The channel especially is scraped, slightly deepened and thoroughly refined right up to, but not beyond, the 2 mm limit from the edge. Pay particular attention to the *rounded* ending of the channel in the corners.

With the main shop lights off, and the windows shaded if necessary, use the adjustable swing arm **bench light** to show up by shadows any irregularities in the arched surface. Satisfy yourself that the arching is right; once we have graduated the back, we can't change it much.

HOLLOWING THE BACK

Mark the flat surface of the back with a pencil gauge 7 mm in from the edge except at the blocks. Continue this line smoothly in a guitar shape across the corners. Draw a straight line across at the inside edges of the upper and lower blocks as shown in the **full size drawing**. These lines reserve the **flat gluing area** for the blocks and linings. All hollowing and graduation must be done within this boundary.

[Another way to mark out this area for hollowing is to temporarily clamp the finished rib assembly in place on the back and trace around the inside of the linings and blocks with a pencil. The alignment pins are helpful. This is the easier and *more accurate* way to do it, but to do it we would have to jump ahead to THE BODY chapter, and first remove the mold and finish the inside of the rib assembly before tracing from it. In either case avoid hollowing outside the straight lines at the upper and lower blocks.]

Set up your **drill press** as a *graduating drill* for a preliminary 5 mm thickness overall. The flat end of a dowel set into the drill press table, just under the drill serves as the reference. The back is held with its arched surface flat on this dowel; otherwise you will drill too deep! (Using a flat-ended dowel helps keep the drill perpendicular to the convex arched surface, and is thus more precise. But if you want to drill right in the channel use a round-ended dowel.) Make sure there are no sharp edges on the dowel and use a sharp 2 or 3 mm drill and light pressure to prevent denting the outside arched surface. This is especially important later in

SCRAPING THE CHANNEL

AN IMPROVISED THICKNESS DRILL

drilling the soft spruce front. A set of mechanic's "feeler" gauges is convenient for setting or checking the drill for thickness. Drill sufficient **depth guide holes** (about every 20 mm) for the hollowing operation which follows.

Replace the **back** into the **cradle**, *flat* side up. We now rough out the excess wood, gouging mostly cross grain, and down to the bottom of the guide holes. One can easily get discouraged, faced again with the mass of resistant maple to be excavated. Use a sharp, long shanked gouge for power, control, and to avoid skinning your knuckles. Take long, shallow cuts, resharpen when the gouge slows down, and it's not unpleasant — but I wouldn't want to do it every day.

[Of course there are ways, more or less satisfactory, to rough out this excess wood with power tools, but these are outside the scope of this book. The use of a router bit in the drill press in place of the graduating drill naturally comes to mind, but is dangerous for the wood and the operator. Even if you take very light cuts, the bit can grab the wood out of your control in milliseconds.]

GRADUATING THE BACK

See also *Art & Method of the Violin Maker*, pages 52-54. The drawing below is taken from this reference. The back graduation contour lines (on the left) are similar to those on the **full size drawing**, and on your half pattern. (P indicates post, C indicates channel.)

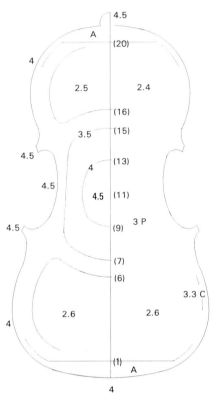

GRADUATION MAP, BACK AND FRONT

Mark these on the back through the perforations in the aluminum half pattern. Use the **graduating drill** and a graduation **map** traced from the **full size drawing** to drill guide holes in the roughly hollowed back according to the specified thickness *contours* and *zones*. (You may wish to set the drill a little shallow for safety at first.)

Using fairly flat **gouges**, round bottomed thumb **planes**, and **scrapers**, work down *almost* to the *bottom* of the guide holes. Smoothly and gradually blend the different thicknesses, frequently checking with the **graduating caliper**, and shadow testing with the bench **light** as you did for the outside arching. Check also by sliding the back between thumb and forefinger. This "natural caliper" is very sensitive to irregularities in thickness.

[The areas marked A at the upper and lower blocks should be left flat all across, but some makers continue the hollowing right up to the sides of the blocks.]

Please note: The graduation of the back (and much more so of the front), has a major effect on the "tone" of the violin. The graduation described here is typical

and will likely result in an acceptable violin, but the final tone character will depend on the wood characteristics, our experience in making and adjusting — and everything else.

The perceptive master maker can more or less predictably make good sounding instruments. But no one can say *exactly* how to "tune" the parts of someone else's violin. There are too many variables in model and procedure to be able to prescribe a simple recipe for success. Perhaps in a tightly specified factory process, using wood selected for plainness and uniformity, but this is not my intention here!

In general, a violin that is too thin may sound hollow or "tubby." One that is too thick will be "uptight" or harsh, but this can be corrected.

If you're new to this, I suggest you follow the procedure here, keep records of your actual graduations and tap tones, do clean work and don't graduate *too* thin. Your violin will likely sound fine, and your next one better. Even if it doesn't sound good, but *looks* good, you or someone else will eventually be able to take it apart and make it *sound*.

GRADUATING DIAL CALIPERS
(ALSO SHOWN ARE VERNIER AND "THROUGH THE SOUND HOLE" CALIPERS)

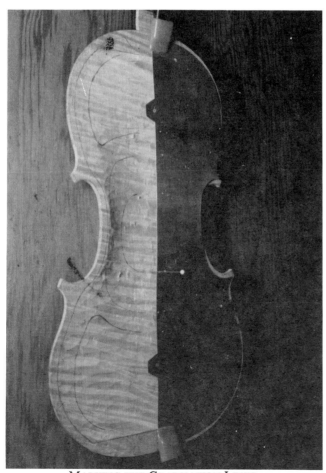

MARKING THE GRADUATION LINES

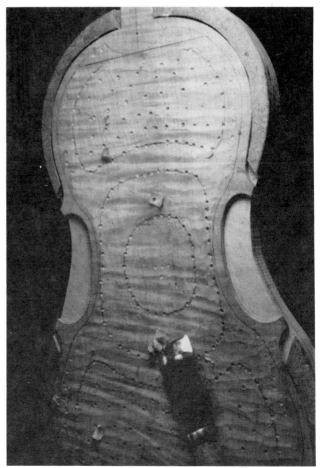

GRADUATION GUIDE HOLES IN THE BACK

TAP TONES

I think that from the beginning violin makers have *tapped and listened* to the resonant tones of the wood as they worked. And good repairers always do this in rebarring when they listen for a tap tone around F.

There is not just one tap tone. Physical bodies, including strings, bars, plates and membranes, vibrate in different patterns or *modes* at different frequencies. These "Chladni figures" were observed by the 19th C. researcher of that name by sprinkling sand on things and vibrating them. Some modern violin makers use a similar method to test the vibrations of the back and front separate from the instrument. For example, a loudspeaker vibrates the plate while lightweight particles show the pattern of vibration by forming *nodal* lines of least movement. Exactly what this means for a particular whole violin is not quite clear, but it could be useful as a production control or inspection procedure.

Various wood and air vibrations of the whole violin have also been studied. Experienced practitioners have promoted specific procedures and criteria. In fact serious research into violin acoustics has gone on in various countries for the last 60 years or so. The clearing house for this information is the international Catgut Acoustical Society. For their address and others see page 33 of *Useful Measurements for Violin Makers*.

We have a better understanding of how violins work from this cumulative study, but I feel that some of the highly touted electronic tuning procedures do not conveniently mesh with traditional violin making, and seem even less appropriate in repair and restoration, where they might easily be misused. They seem unnecessarily complicated and restrictive, and perhaps raise more questions than answers. However helpful to some, they are obviously *not essential* for good violin making, and are not used by a majority of professional makers.

The expert professional maker derives his direction from his experience and from examining the graduation, barring, tap tones, adjustment, and sound of good violins.

Every maker ought to know something about **tap tones**. They provide a working frame of reference. To *hear* a tap tone, *hold* the back (or front) plate of the violin between thumb and finger at a point along a nodal line, for example, **H5** in the drawing below. Bring it close to the ear and *tap* at **T5** with a finger tip of the other hand. You may have to experiment a bit to get exactly on the nodal line for the clearest tone. Hum the tone you hear into a hands free electronic **tuner**. (In a quiet room some tuners can directly pick up the sound.) This

will give the note and what percentage of a semitone sharp or flat it is. Lacking a tuner, you can approximately identify these tap tones with a piano, or with your own perfect pitch.

Mode 5 is the most important tap tone for the violin maker. It has an "O"-shaped nodal line, which of course you will not *see* unless you use the Chladni apparatus. Hold at **H5** and tap at **T5**. This tap tone is in octave number 4 of the piano, just above middle C. (The back I have just finished graduating has a tone of about F+20 cents, which I note for future reference.)

There are at least two other tap tones that may be of interest. The different tones are sometimes confused, so here is how to distinguish them:

Mode 2 has an "X"-shaped nodal pattern. Hold at **H2** and tap at **T2**. This is in octave number 3 of the piano.

Mode 1 has a "+"-shaped nodal pattern . Hold at **H1** and tap at **T1**. This is in octave number 2 of the piano.

(If you are interested, this back I have just graduated has its mode 2 at D+25 and mode 1 at G#-40 cents. I am not going to worry about these. The lower mode 2 is typical for this graduation pattern and wood, but my experience with it has been good. I also note that in our method here the edges are still square and heavy. They will be rounded and the channel given a final scraping only after the body is assembled. Varnishing will raise the tone too, so let's not go overboard on details.)

This drawing shows examples of *approximately* where to hold and where to tap for these three modes in the back or front. Many other locations along the nodal lines will work, but let's keep it simple.

For more information about **musical intervals** and **frequencies** please see page 52-57 of *Violin Maker's Notebook*, especially the Frequency Table, page 56.

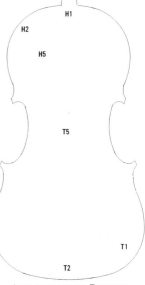

APPROXIMATE POINTS
TO HOLD & TAP

Now let's set the **back** safely aside while we proceed to prepare the *front* of our violin.

You will have noticed that I am using the good English word *front* instead of *top*, *table*, *belly*, *breast*, or *soundboard*. It seems simpler.

Many of the steps in making the **front** are the same as those used in making the **back**, and you can refer to the previous chapter when necessary. The **wood** and the **graduation** are different. And we have to add the **soundholes** and **bass bar**.

THE FRONT WOOD

Select a straight grained piece of European spruce (*picea abies*), or *Engelmann*, *Sitka*, or *red* spruce from North America. The late wood (dark lines) should be preferably thin and their spacing neither very wide nor extremely narrow. The grain must be vertical. If the wood is sawed out instead of split, make a small test split in the waste area to be sure there is little *runout* of the grain.

JOINING THE FRONT (See THE BACK.)

TRACING THE OUTLINE (See THE BACK.)

The (optional) **alignment pins** at the upper and lower blocks are placed a little differently for the front than for the back. After clamping the front to the upper and lower blocks, drill the 1 mm holes through the front and into the blocks preferably within the areas that will later be cut away for the neck mortise and the saddle, that is, on the line of the future purfling. These holes will be very close to the ribs, so you may decide to

USING A THUMB PLANE IN SPRUCE

them later, or simply omit them, as I do.

CUTTING OUT THE FRONT (See THE BACK.)

PRELIMINARY ARCHING (See THE BACK.)

Compared to the maple, carving the spruce is sheer pleasure. But use care not to split out large pieces. And we have to have, if anything, even *sharper* tools to cleanly do the finish work below. This is especially true for scrapers.

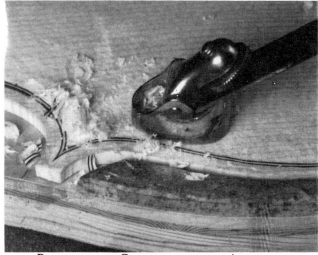

BLENDING THE CHANNEL INTO THE ARCHING
(THE PURFLING CHIPS WERE CUT BY THE GOUGE.)

PURFLING (See THE BACK.)

The work here too is easier compared to the back, but the hard grain lines tend to deflect the knife from its intended path. Use a sharp knife, of course. It may help to first cut straight down into some of the grain lines rather than just plowing into them from the side.

[It's unnecessary, but some find it helpful to pretreat the groove area with *thin* glue to give a more uniform surface for marking and cutting the groove. Clean off any excess and let thoroughly dry first.]

FINAL ARCHING (See THE BACK.)

It is even more important on the **spruce front** for the **planes** and **scrapers** to be really *sharp*. Rough planing across the grain is usual, but finish planing and scraping should be more or less *with* the grain. Planing against the grain may lift large splinters out; scraping straight across digs into the soft grain.

See MARKING THE SOUNDHOLES below for special arching considerations at arching guides F2 and F3.

See also CUTTING THE SOUND HOLES below for the special sculpting of the lower wings of the **sound holes**.

Use care now in scraping as you are essentially making the final wood surface, although you will probably do another light clean-up scraping just before varnishing. Spruce is a plain looking wood, and we would like to end up with an attractive "reedy" or "corduroy" texture and coloring.

Final scraping with a *slightly* dull scraper will cut the resistant, hard, dark grain lines but just compress the compliant, soft, light wood between. (Sanding, on the other hand, can have the opposite effect.) When you dampen the wood before applying the ground, this soft wood will further swell out, leaving the dark grain lines as recessed grooves. When varnishing, the color will lie thicker in these grooves, enhancing the appearance and texture of the grain.

[If you don't care about this, you can sand it all smooth, but your violin will look less "hand carved."]

ENGELMANN SPRUCE AFTER PRELIMINARY SCRAPING

HOLLOWING THE FRONT (See THE BACK.)

Set the drill for a preliminary thickness of 3.6 mm for the front (instead of the 5 mm we used for the back). But do not drill in the area between the sound holes and the edge. Leave this a little thick until later to allow for the final sculpting after the sound holes are cut. This area is often made too thin, thus weak and susceptible to wing cracks and sound post setter damage.

MARKING THE SOUND HOLES

See also *Art & Method of the Violin Maker*, page 56.

Lightly **mark** the line of the *"stop"* with a pencil across the front 195 mm from the upper edge. This line locates the line of the inner notches of the soundholes, which will in turn later locate the centerline of the bridge.

Note: Many makers feel that the soundholes, seen from the side of the violin, should appear parallel to the edge, and not run "downhill" toward it. Our model violin passes this test, but it is not a necessary criterion. It does imply that the arching should rise rather rapidly at arching guide 3, and not too rapidly at arching guide 2. See the photograph.

SOUND HOLE, SIDE VIEW (BISIACH)

(Continued on page 43)

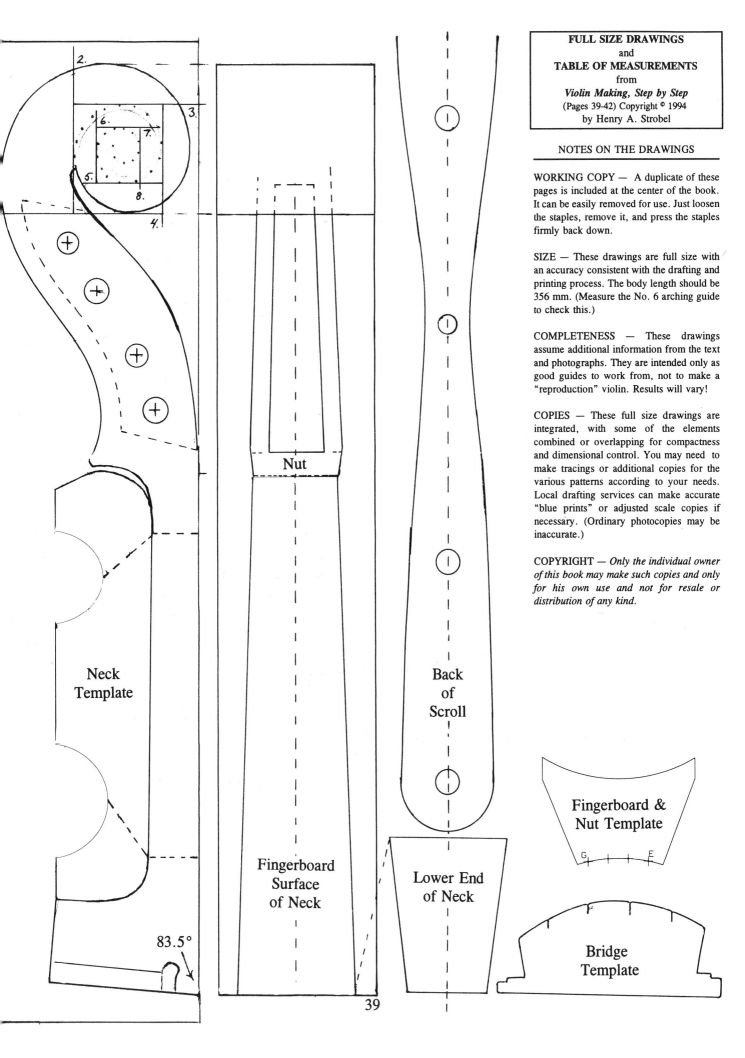

NOTES ON THE DRAWINGS

WORKING COPY — A duplicate of these pages is included at the center of the book. It can be easily removed for use. Just loosen the staples, remove it, and press the staples firmly back down.

SIZE — These drawings are full size with an accuracy consistent with the drafting and printing process. The body length should be 356 mm. (Measure the No. 6 arching guide to check this.)

COMPLETENESS — These drawings assume additional information from the text and photographs. They are intended only as good guides to work from, not to make a "reproduction" violin. Results will vary!

COPIES — These full size drawings are integrated, with some of the elements combined or overlapping for compactness and dimensional control. You may need to make tracings or additional copies for the various patterns according to your needs. Local drafting services can make accurate "blue prints" or adjusted scale copies if necessary. (Ordinary photocopies may be inaccurate.)

Neck Template

Nut

Fingerboard Surface of Neck

83.5°

Back of Scroll

Lower End of Neck

Fingerboard & Nut Template

Bridge Template

39

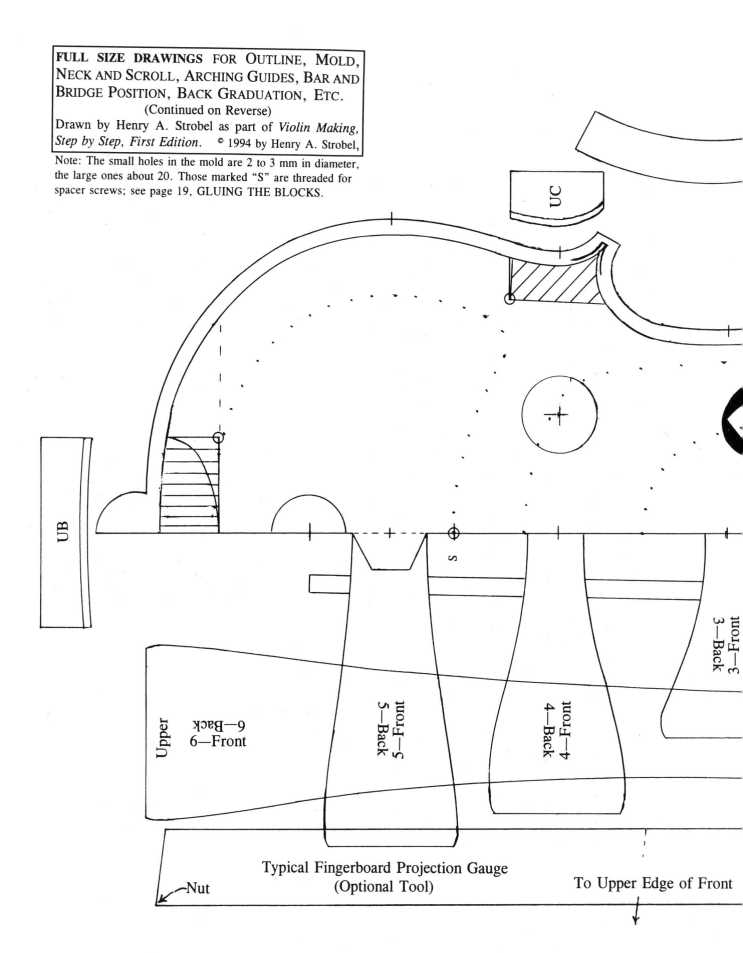

UC

UB

3—Front
3—Back

Upper
6—Back
6—Front

5—Front
5—Back

4—Front
4—Back

S

Typical Fingerboard Projection Gauge
(Optional Tool)

Nut

To Upper Edge of Front

40

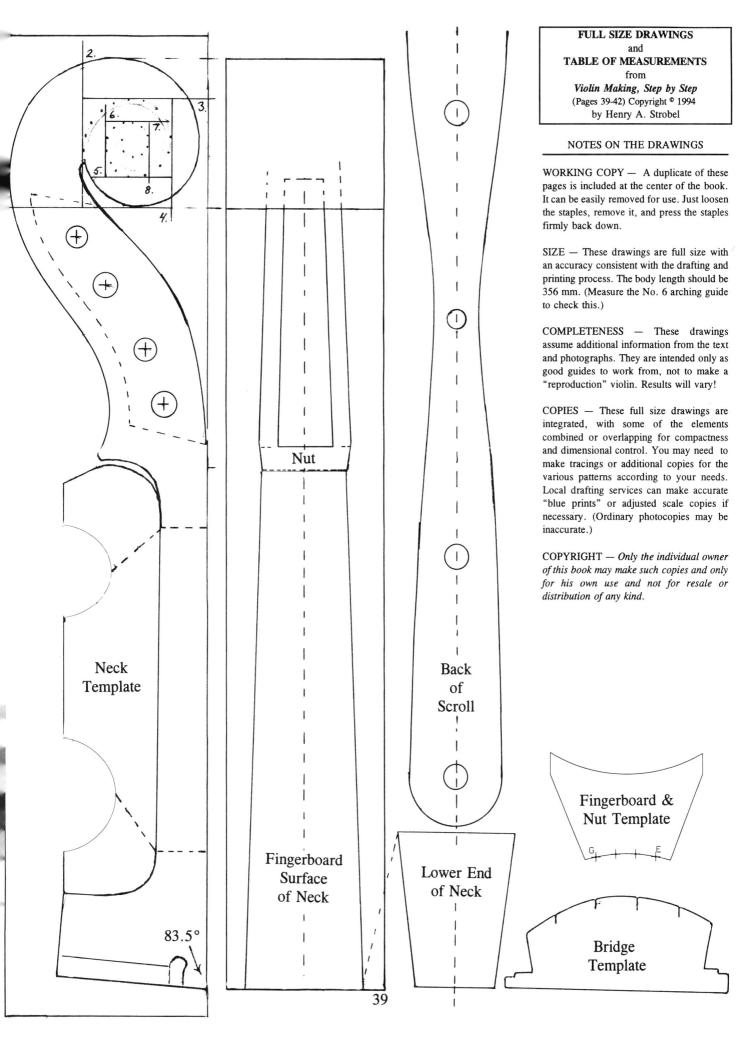

FULL SIZE DRAWINGS
and
TABLE OF MEASUREMENTS
from
Violin Making, Step by Step
(Pages 39-42) Copyright © 1994
by Henry A. Strobel

NOTES ON THE DRAWINGS

WORKING COPY — A duplicate of these pages is included at the center of the book. It can be easily removed for use. Just loosen the staples, remove it, and press the staples firmly back down.

SIZE — These drawings are full size with an accuracy consistent with the drafting and printing process. The body length should be 356 mm. (Measure the No. 6 arching guide to check this.)

COMPLETENESS — These drawings assume additional information from the text and photographs. They are intended only as good guides to work from, not to make a "reproduction" violin. Results will vary!

COPIES — These full size drawings are integrated, with some of the elements combined or overlapping for compactness and dimensional control. You may need to make tracings or additional copies for the various patterns according to your needs. Local drafting services can make accurate "blue prints" or adjusted scale copies if necessary. (Ordinary photocopies may be inaccurate.)

COPYRIGHT — *Only the individual owner of this book may make such copies and only for his own use and not for resale or distribution of any kind.*

Nut

Neck
Template

Fingerboard
Surface
of Neck

83.5°

Back
of
Scroll

Lower End
of Neck

Fingerboard &
Nut Template

Bridge
Template

Note: The small holes in the mold are 2 to 3 mm in diameter,
the large ones about 20. Those marked "S" are threaded for
spacer screws; see page 19, GLUING THE BLOCKS.

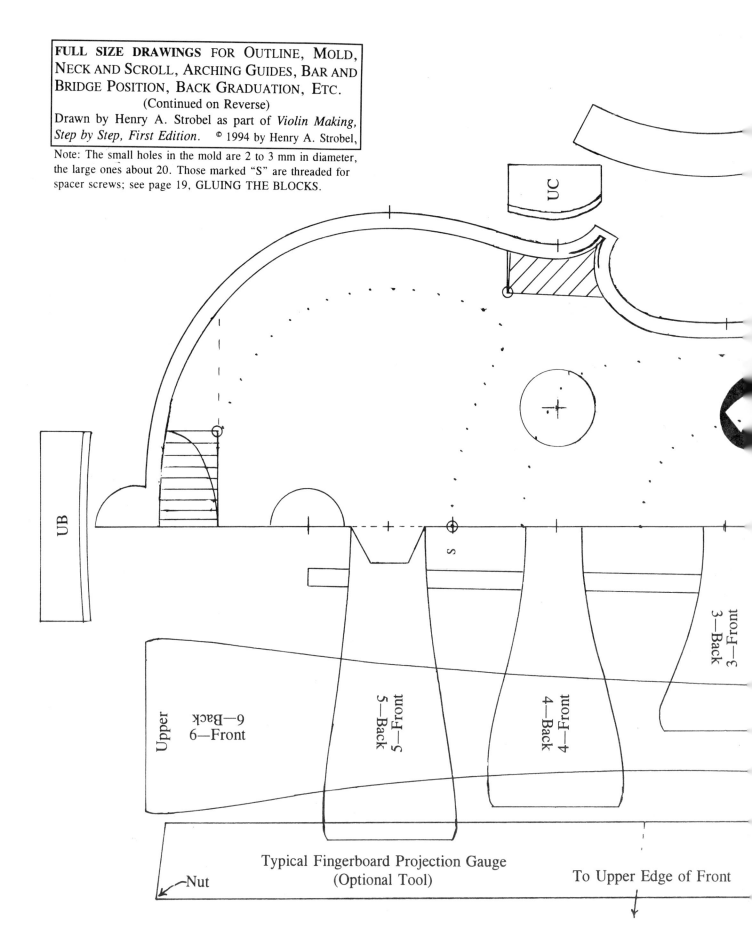

Typical Fingerboard Projection Gauge
(Optional Tool)

Nut

To Upper Edge of Front

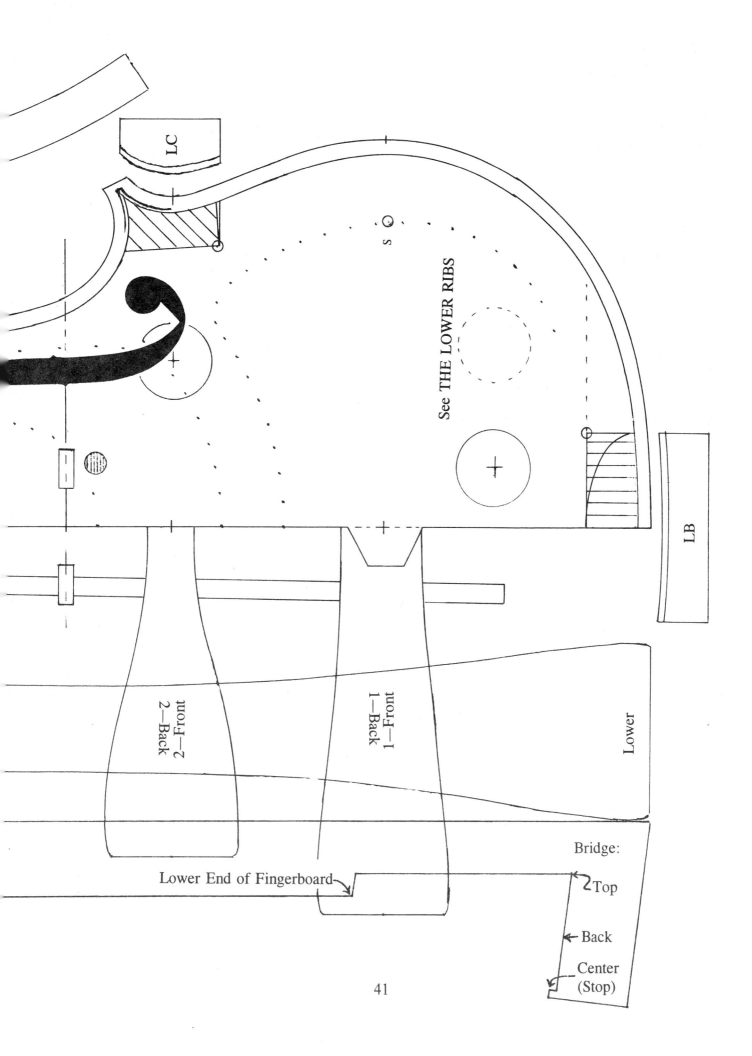

C

See THE LOWER RIBS

S

LB

2—Front
2—Back

1—Front
1—Back

Lower

Lower End of Fingerboard

Bridge:

Top

Back

Center
(Stop)

TABLE OF NOMINAL VIOLIN MEASUREMENTS IN MILLIMETERS Copyright © 1994 Henry A. Strobel

Adapted for *Violin Making, Step by Step* from the tables in the author's *Useful Measurements for Violin Makers*
(To change millimeters to inches, divide by 25.4.)

Body Outline . . . . See Patterns & Photos
Body Length 356
Body Width, Upper 165
Body Width, Middle 108
Body Width, Lower 205

Rib Height at Neck 30
Rib Height at Lower Block 32
Rib Thickness 1
Rib Length, Upper, Preliminary. 180
Rib Length, Middle, Preliminary. 140
Rib Length, Lower, Preliminary. 230

Lining Height, Preliminary 7
Lining Thickness, Preliminary 2
Lining Length, Upper, Preliminary. 150
Lining Length, Middle, Preliminary 120
Lining Length, Lower, Preliminary. 180

Arching Shape . . . . See Patterns & Photos
Arching Height, Front 15.5
Arching Height, Back 15

Soundhole Outline . . . . . See Patterns & Photos
Distance Between Upper Soundhole Circles . 41
Distance Between Lower Soundhole Circles . 112

Air Tone, Complete Instrument (Approximate)   C
Front Tap Tone with Soundholes & Bar.   F to F#
Front Thickness, Upper 2.5
Front Thickness near Post & Soundholes 3
Front Thickness, Elsewhere 2.6
Back Thickness, Upper 2.5
Back Thickness, Middle . . . . 3.4 to 4.5
Back Thickness, Lower 2.6
Thickness in Channel, Front & Back 3.3

Bar Length (150 mm above the stop, 120 below) 270
Bar Width (Before Tuning) 5
Bar Height at Bridge (Approximate) 14
Bar Height at Ends (Approximate) 2

Corner Width & Outline . . See Patterns & Photos
Edge Thickness at Middle, Corners, Button . . 4.5
Edge Thickness, Elsewhere 4
Edge Overhang at Corners 2
Edge Overhang Elsewhere 3
Channel Distance to Edge 2
Purfling Distance to Edge 4
Purfling Groove Depth 2

Upper Edge of Front to Bridge Center 195
Neck Length, Upper Edge of Front to Nut . . . 130
Neck Length, Nut to Lower End of Neck . . . 138
Neck Width at Lower End 32

Neck Height at Lower End (83.5°) 41
Neck Height over Upper Edge of Front 6
Neck Thickness, Upper, Without Fingerboard   13
Neck Thickness, Lower, Without Fingerboard   14
Neck Thickness, Upper, With Fingerboard . . 19
Neck Thickness, Lower, With Fingerboard . . 21
Back Button Width 21
Back Button Length 13

Scroll & Neck Outline . . . See Patterns & Photos
Scroll Width 42
Width of Scroll Chamfer (Bevel) 1.5
Pegbox Width, Upper Inside 10
Pegbox Width, Lower, Lower Inside 15
Pegbox Side Thickness at Opening 5
Pegbox Side Thickness at Back 6

Peg Hole Spacing, E to G and A to D 15
Peg Hole Spacing, E to D 20
Pegbox to Inside Edge of Thumbpiece 15
Peg End Finish Radius 20

Nut Length at Pegbox Opening 25
Nut Length at Fingerboard 23.5
Nut Height over Fingerboard 0.5
Nut Width, Underside 6

Saddle Height 7.5
Saddle Width 36

Fingerboard Length 270
Fingerboard Width at Nut 23.5
Fingerboard Width at Lower End 42
Fingerboard Edge Thickness on G Side . . . 5.5
Fingerboard Edge Thickness on E Side 4.7
Fingerboard Surface Radius of Curvature . . . 42
Fingerboard Surface Concavity under E String 0.5
Fingerboard Surface Concavity under G String 0.7
Fingerboard Height Projected to Bridge 27

String E to G Spacing at Nut 16.3
String E to G Spacing at Bridge 33.5
(Divide into 3 equal parts along arc for A and D.)

E String Clearance over End of Fingerboard . . 3
G String Clearance over End of Fingerboard . 5.5
String Clearance over Fingerboard at Nut . . . 0.3
Groove Depth, Nut & Bridge: 1/3 String Diameter
Groove Width, Nut & Bridge: 1/2 String Diameter

Bridge Width at Feet 41
Bridge Thickness at Strings 1.3
Bridge Thickness at Feet 4.2
Bridge Foot Height 1.0
Sound Post Diameter 6

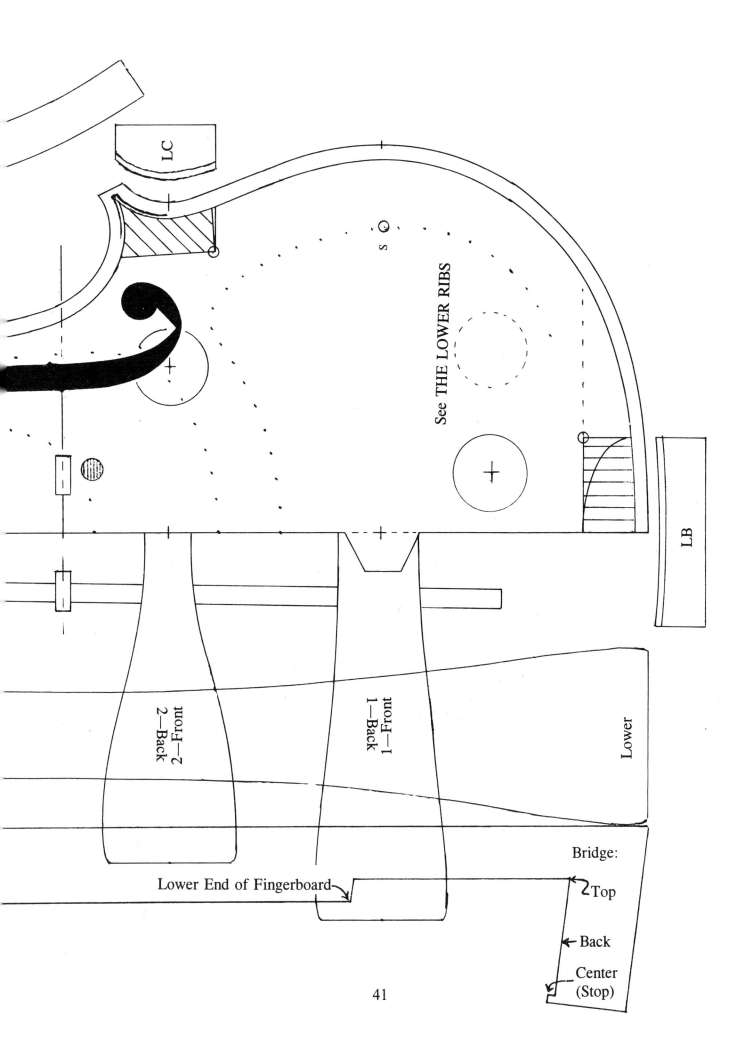

See THE LOWER RIBS

LC

LB

2—Front
2—Back

1—Front
1—Back

Lower

Lower End of Fingerboard

Bridge:

Top

Back

Center
(Stop)

41

Adapted for *Violin Making, Step by Step* from the tables in the author's *Useful Measurements for Violin Makers*
(To change millimeters to inches, divide by 25.4.)

Body Outline . . . . See Patterns & Photos
Body Length 356
Body Width, Upper 165
Body Width, Middle 108
Body Width, Lower 205

Rib Height at Neck 30
Rib Height at Lower Block 32
Rib Thickness 1
Rib Length, Upper, Preliminary. 180
Rib Length, Middle, Preliminary. 140
Rib Length, Lower, Preliminary. 230

Lining Height, Preliminary 7
Lining Thickness, Preliminary 2
Lining Length, Upper, Preliminary. 150
Lining Length, Middle, Preliminary 120
Lining Length, Lower, Preliminary. 180

Arching Shape . . . . See Patterns & Photos
Arching Height, Front 15.5
Arching Height, Back 15

Soundhole Outline . . . . . See Patterns & Photos
Distance Between Upper Soundhole Circles . 41
Distance Between Lower Soundhole Circles . 112

Air Tone, Complete Instrument (Approximate) C
Front Tap Tone with Soundholes & Bar. F to F#
Front Thickness, Upper 2.5
Front Thickness near Post & Soundholes 3
Front Thickness, Elsewhere 2.6
Back Thickness, Upper 2.5
Back Thickness, Middle . . . . 3.4 to 4.5
Back Thickness, Lower 2.6
Thickness in Channel, Front & Back 3.3

Bar Length (150 mm above the stop, 120 below) 270
Bar Width (Before Tuning) 5
Bar Height at Bridge (Approximate) 14
Bar Height at Ends (Approximate) 2

Corner Width & Outline . . See Patterns & Photos
Edge Thickness at Middle, Corners, Button . . 4.5
Edge Thickness, Elsewhere 4
Edge Overhang at Corners 2
Edge Overhang Elsewhere 3
Channel Distance to Edge 2
Purfling Distance to Edge 4
Purfling Groove Depth 2

Upper Edge of Front to Bridge Center 195
Neck Length, Upper Edge of Front to Nut . . . 130
Neck Length, Nut to Lower End of Neck . . . 138
Neck Width at Lower End 32

Neck Height at Lower End (83.5°) 41
Neck Height over Upper Edge of Front 6
Neck Thickness, Upper, Without Fingerboard 13
Neck Thickness, Lower, Without Fingerboard 14
Neck Thickness, Upper, With Fingerboard . . 19
Neck Thickness, Lower, With Fingerboard . . 21
Back Button Width 21
Back Button Length 13

Scroll & Neck Outline . . . See Patterns & Photos
Scroll Width 42
Width of Scroll Chamfer (Bevel) 1.5
Pegbox Width, Upper Inside 10
Pegbox Width, Lower, Lower Inside 15
Pegbox Side Thickness at Opening 5
Pegbox Side Thickness at Back 6

Peg Hole Spacing, E to G and A to D 15
Peg Hole Spacing, E to D 20
Pegbox to Inside Edge of Thumbpiece 15
Peg End Finish Radius 20

Nut Length at Pegbox Opening 25
Nut Length at Fingerboard 23.5
Nut Height over Fingerboard 0.5
Nut Width, Underside 6

Saddle Height 7.5
Saddle Width 36

Fingerboard Length 270
Fingerboard Width at Nut 23.5
Fingerboard Width at Lower End 42
Fingerboard Edge Thickness on G Side 5.5
Fingerboard Edge Thickness on E Side 4.7
Fingerboard Surface Radius of Curvature . . . 42
Fingerboard Surface Concavity under E String 0.5
Fingerboard Surface Concavity under G String 0.7
Fingerboard Height Projected to Bridge 27

String E to G Spacing at Nut 16.3
String E to G Spacing at Bridge 33.5
(Divide into 3 equal parts along arc for A and D.)

E String Clearance over End of Fingerboard . . 3
G String Clearance over End of Fingerboard . 5.5
String Clearance over Fingerboard at Nut . . . 0.3
Groove Depth, Nut & Bridge: 1/3 String Diameter
Groove Width, Nut & Bridge: 1/2 String Diameter

Bridge Width at Feet 41
Bridge Thickness at Strings 1.3
Bridge Thickness at Feet 4.2
Bridge Foot Height 1.0
Sound Post Diameter 6

42

(Continued from page 38)

The **soundhole template** is best made of thin, transparent plastic taped to the **full size drawing** and precisely cut out with a knife. Align it to the centerline of the drawing and accurately scribe the line of the stop on the pattern. (Do not trace the template from the photograph on the right.)

Please note that the sound hole on the **full size drawing** is traced from the arched surface, and so is wider than would appear looking straight down on the violin plan. It also looks closer to the edge in the drawing than it will be on the violin because of the arching. I have shown this variation from flat to arched in the extra line at the outside edge of the template photograph here.

The finished pattern is now placed on the front, aligned with the centerline and stop. Check that the lower sound hole circle looks right as placed, with an approximate separation from the edge of 11-12 mm (on this model). This is different than the **full size drawing**, on which the sound hole pattern is shown *flat*.

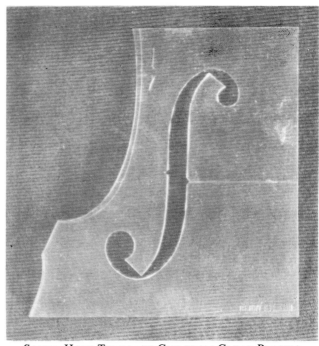

SOUND HOLE TEMPLATE CUT FROM CLEAR PLASTIC
(FLIPPED OVER FROM THE FULL SIZE DRAWING HERE)

RIGHT SOUNDHOLE, BISIACH

LEFT SOUNDHOLE, BISIACH
(NOTE THE BAR LOCATION)

THE ENSEMBLE, BISIACH

Tape the pattern in place and mark around the inside of its cutout in pencil. This pencil line will be removed in cutting the soundhole, or the hole will finish too narrow. If the holes are too narrow the sound will be poor; it will also be difficult to install or extract a fallen post. Remove, flip the pattern, and mark the other soundhole.

CUTTING THE SOUND HOLES

The soundholes can be cut out completely with a **knife**, but we will find it convenient to drill undersized **starting holes** in the centers of the upper and lower circles and between the notches. You may also prefer to connect the upper and lower circles with a small **saw blade** in a handle. The remaining wood will be cut out to the pattern line with a **knife** and, if you like, files. The sides of the soundholes should be cut *square* with the front surface.

[Special clean cutting sound hole circle cutters with a central guide pin are available. This is an excellent way to do it. We could use these, we could also use a jig saw or coping saw, but we do not *need* them.]

[Before making the finishing cuts with the knife and round file, you may want to *seal* the cutting surface with very *thin*, light and clear hide **glue**. Keep it off the front, and let it dry before cutting. This can also make the delicate wing tips a little less fragile.]

We now refine the modelling of the lower wing of the soundholes, scraping it slightly concave and blending this gracefully into the arching to the outside of the soundholes. This effect has come to be expected, but it is too often overdone, occasionally becoming a caricature. Keep it subtle and graceful. Study this on a fine violin, if possible.

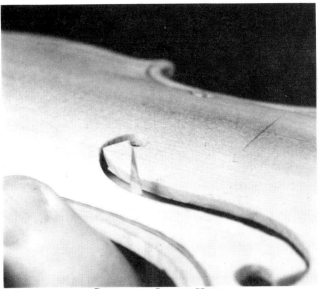

CUTTING A SOUND HOLE

GRADUATING THE FRONT (See also THE BACK.)

The *front* **graduation** we will use is very simple, essentially uniform, except for the slightly thicker areas, which provide strength around the post and soundholes, especially their lower wings, and are blended smoothly into the rest.

If you have very stiff wood and want to simply use the thicknesses attributed to Stradivari by Sacconi, you can proceed directly and use the graduating drill as follows:

3.3 mm thickness along the channel (just inside the purfling).
2.7 mm all around the sound holes, and in a 22 mm circle at the post.
2.6 mm elsewhere, except in the area above the upper corners, where it is reduced to 2.4.

But beware; these are too *thin* for most wood, and certainly for the wood I am using in this violin, which is Engelmann Spruce that was cut about 30 years ago, pretty but *very light*. Also, making the thickness only 0.1 mm greater at the soundholes and post is hardly enough to make a significant difference, and is in the measurement error range.

I graduated with "educated intuition," and this front, before barring, is now about 3.4 mm in the center and at the sound holes, 2.7 to 3.3 elsewhere. This is of course thicker than normal, but this is light wood, and I prefer conservatism at this point.

I am going to be deliberately vague about front tap tones here for these reasons: The wood I am using is not typical, and I have no reason to recommend these particular values. For the record, to the nearest semitone, the front tones now *happen* to be:

Mode 5: D   Octave number 4
Mode 2: C#   Octave number 3
Mode 1: E   Octave number 2

[There are other successful graduation schemes given and observed elsewhere, thicker in the middle and thinner toward the edges, for example. That's up to you.]

BARRING

See *Art & Method of the Violin Maker*, pages 57-58.

The size and location of a typical **bar** for our violin are given in the **full size drawings**. Mark its **location** inside the **front** with light pencil marks. (The usual rule is to divide the upper and lower maximum widths by 7 and measure from the centerline to find the angle and approximate location.) In the present case, we will measure down 45 mm from the top of the front and 40 mm up from the bottom to locate the upper and lower ends of the bar, which are 11 mm and 15 mm from the centerline respectively.

It's a good idea to clamp the front into the cradle to hold the edges flat while fitting the bar, since the front is now quite flexible. Select a piece of spruce with thin, close annual rings, with the same direction as those in the front. Plane it to a uniform thickness of 5 mm. Fit it *approximately* to the inside arching of the front with knife and plane.

Then, with a pencil and washer (or a nut as in the photo), gauge the inside front curve onto both sides of the bar. Plane this accurately to both lines. Chalk the

MARKING THE BAR

GLUING THE BAR WITH SPECIAL CORK-LINED CLAMPS,
ONE OF MANY SUITABLE CLAMPING ARRANGEMENTS

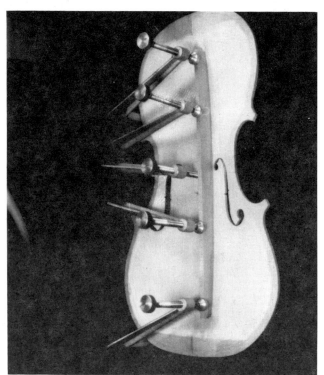

THE CLAMPS INSIDE (THE MIDDLE CLAMP HOLDS A
BLOCK TO PREVENT THE BAR FROM SLIDING.)

area previously marked out on the inside of the front. Place the bar on this and rub it back and forth 1 or 2 mm. This will mark any high spots on the bar, which are then planed off with a block plane set for a very thin cut (or filed, if you prefer). Repeat as necessary; when the bar fits perfectly, glue it in place. Given the flexibility of the front plate, we will probably end up with 1 or 2 mm of space between the ends of the bar and the front plate, even though it is well fitted. This is called the "spring" of the bar and this amount is usually OK.

Use either improvised wood "U"-shaped clamps or lightweight aluminum adjustable clamps, well padded with cork at the front. Use light clamping force and not too much water in washing off the glue; let it dry overnight.

[Wooden cam type clamps are also a convenient alternative. If you do use heavy metal clamps, rest these on the bench, with the violin front vertical, to avoid distortion.]

The bar is still more or less rectangular in section and too high. In general, a higher, thinner bar is better than a lower, wider one for a given tap tone. The greatest height is at the bridge and along the sound holes, and somewhat lower toward the upper end than the lower. Trim away the obviously excess wood with gouge or knife before beginning the careful process of final trimming and shaping, which actually *tunes* the front to its desired stiffness and pitch. Use a flat bottomed thumb plane for this.

Setting the *tap tone* (mode 5) of the front of the violin with the bass bar is a traditional adjustment. When you do this, be sure that the glue has thoroughly dried — at least overnight, since the tone will be higher when it's dry. Carefully monitor this tap tone as you trim (tune) the bar down to it. It will be from E to F#, depending on the *tonality* (dark or bright) wanted.

There can't be a rule, but many would agree that a front with modes 1, 2, and 5 all about F (in their respective octaves) would not be a bad example. Write the actual tones down for future reference. But remember that if in the future you open the violin and recheck the tones, they will in general be different because of the completed edgework and varnish.

[In this front, after barring, modes 1 and 2 were rather low, about E, but I left the bar high with mode 5 about F. Wondering about this, I borrowed a pepper shaker from the kitchen (to display the nodal lines) and set up the plate tuning apparatus I had made years ago but rarely used. My early impression quickly returned — "I don't have a pretty mode 5 line, but I'm not convinced I need one." I think many good violins do not, depending on their construction method.

The photo below is included *only* for personal historical interest. I designed and built this working prototype about 1980. Note that it is calibrated in semitones and *cents*, not *Herz*. It was not manufactured and is not available.]

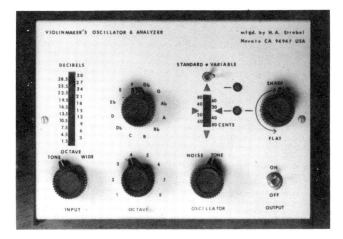

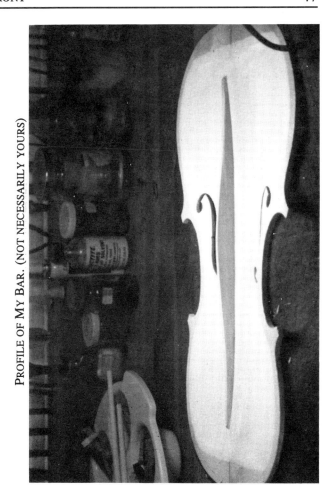

PROFILE OF MY BAR. (NOT NECESSARILY YOURS)

There are various opinions on the location, cross section, and profile of the bar, and probably most of these are not "wrong." Most feel that the greatest height should be at or a little above the bridge line and remain high along the length of the soundholes. Also please refer to pages 57-58 of *Art & Method of the Violin Maker*.

You can see in the photo the profile of this bar. It is high (14 mm) and narrow (about 3 mm on top). Yours will probably differ. More typical bars are 10 -12 mm high. We measure this height on the side nearer the centerline. It will be similar on either side if the bar was fitted perpendicular to the front; there will be a difference in the middle on highly arched fronts, where it is not practical to fit it perpendicular.

[Some makers use a rule of thumb to decrease the height of the bar linearly from the maximum to each end. The height is calculated as if it were not curved.]

Now let's set the **front** safely aside as we finish preparing the **rib assembly** to glue on the back and front.

REMOVING THE MOLD

We have left the blocked and lined rib assembly securely glued to the mold up till now for stability. We obviously have to remove it before we can finish the blocks and close the body. This is not as hard as it may seem if we are careful.

First complete the beveling of the linings with the knife. A simple, straight bevel is best, tapering to a knife edge at the rib. The thumb or finger is placed on the back of the blade and serves as a stop gauge to keep from cutting into the rib.

Then loosen the blocks from the mold, using a small hammer to cautiously break the glue joints. I find that these pop away from the mold easily and cleanly if the mold was sealed with spirit varnish as we recommended when making it. If they do not, you can take the time to unglue them with hot water, or split them away with a chisel in the waste area of the block. With chisels and gouges cut and/or split away most of the excess wood. This will allow us to carefully pull the *middle* ribs away from the mold, expanding the rib assembly enough to remove it. It may take a little oblique maneuvering, but it's not difficult.

[If this proves too stressful for the ribs (or for you), next time you can remove the mold before gluing in the second set of linings, or use **a collapsible three layer mold**.

See *Art & Method of the Violin Maker*, pages 30-33 on inside molds. All three types of inside molds have advantages and disadvantages. We have used the simple, thin **one layer mold** in this book.

The **two layer mold** is the full rib height, held together with screws. One layer is removed after gluing on the ribs to allow the installation of one set of linings, before or after gluing the back on.

The **three layer mold** is interesting but overly complicated. The layers can be conveniently assembled and disassembled using wood screws, or machine screws either threaded into the wood or with "T- nuts" for durability, and countersunk flat head machine screws.

The three layers are first assembled, and the blocks are glued to the *middle* layer. The blocks are shaped and the ribs, which are held perpendicular by the full height mold, are glued in place. The front layer is removed and the front set of linings are installed. (Machine screws are turned into the front layer to separate it.) Now rectangular wood cross ties are installed to hold the collapsible middle layer rigid.

Now the back layer can likewise be removed and the back linings installed and trimmed. The completed ribs can now be glued to the back with the middle layer of the mold still in place, giving stability to the rib assembly.

After gluing the ribs to the back, the rectangular cross ties and the halves of the middle layer are removed. However, it is only now that we can complete shaping the inside of the blocks.]

THE BLOCKS ARE MARKED

MARKING THE LOWER BLOCK

SEE HOW EASILY THE MOLD SLIPS OUT. (THE BLOCKS
HAD BEEN TRIMMED BEFORE THIS PHOTOGRAPH.)

FINISHING THE INSIDE

We now have full access to neatly finish the linings
with the knife, and the blocks with chisel and gouges
(preferably outside beveled for the upper and lower,
inside beveled for the corner blocks). We could further
finish with files, scrapers, sanding blocks, etc., but
there is no need to if we do clean work.

GLUING THE BACK ON

[Before gluing the back on you can, if you prefer, round the edge
of the back that goes toward the ribs. First a bevel is formed with
a knife or file or sanding block. A half round file, or sandpaper
on a dowel, is used in the concave curves near the corners. This
bevel is then "rounded." But stay away from the back button, and
don't round the corners! I prefer to leave this step until after the
back and front are glued on. This makes it easier to adjust the
overhang margins while gluing and later. And it can readily be
done without damaging the rib surfaces if you are careful.]

The back should be more securely glued on than the
front, which has to be more easily removable. Use hot,
regular strength glue. The end grain of the blocks tend

to soak up glue, so first brush it liberally on these and
wipe off the excess.

Insert the snugly fitting **alignment pins** (small brads)
through the previously made holes in the back. Leave
the heads protruding for easy removal with pliers.

[Those that are experienced in hot gluing can go ahead and brush
the glue all around at once, then repeating it on the blocks.]

Otherwise we can proceed more calmly, clamping the
blocks to the back dry and perfectly aligned,
temporarily removing a few clamps and gluing a section
at a time. First brush hot glue on the mating surfaces at
the upper and lower blocks. Promptly align the pins in
the back with the holes in the blocks and apply the
clamps. These blocks are best held in place with small
C clamps, protecting the wood with cork padded wood
clamping blocks. Use ordinary closing (spool) clamps
along the ribs, using great care to keep them vertical.
Inaccuracy here will make it harder to align the front.
If you made scribe marks on the back along the ribs
when you earlier traced the back outline, these can now
be used to help set the overhang margins. Otherwise
you can set the vernier caliper depth gauge to a nominal
3 mm and use this to even the margin all around.

Begin gluing with the corners. Temporarily remove
several adjacent clamps at a time and apply the glue
with a *thin* palette knife. Remove excess glue from the
inside with hot water (not too much to avoid warping)
on a stiff brush followed by a paper towel. After the
glue has partially set, remove excess glue from the
outside, temporarily removing one or two clamps at a
time. Be thorough; residual glue can interfere with the
varnishing process.

If you have used alignment pins that have left visible
holes, plug these with decorative dowels, 1 to 2 mm in
diameter. The choice of wood is yours. (There's
nothing wrong with round birch toothpicks.) It's better
to keep them short of the blocks. Otherwise they are
structural, but more awkward if the back has to be
removed for some reason.

THE LABEL

Now it's almost time to glue in our **label**. But first let's
inspect the whole interior to see if there's further
scraping, smoothing, or tidying up to do before we
close it up. Interior coatings are not considered here,
but we may want to polish up the interior a little by dry
rubbing. This gives a slightly shiny, "burnished"
appearance. The **synthetic rubbing mesh** mentioned in
the chapter on varnish is good for this.

[Others have used dried horsetail grass, wood shavings, dried dogfish (sand shark) skin, clean coiled bow hair, etc. to polish the wood inside before closing, or outside before varnishing. (True burnishing with a hard object, inside or outside, has no merit that I know of.)]

What you put on your label is up to you, as long as it's factual. Let's hope it stays there, and is not removed, replaced, or papered over by some distant devious dealer. Use thin hide glue. Place it parallel to the centerline and legible through the left soundhole. You may supplement the label by stamping the wood in various places on the inside. Your **bridge stamp** is suitable for this.

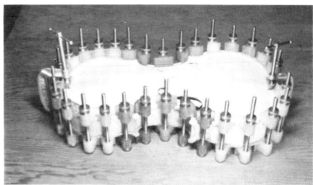

2 C-CLAMPS AND 30 PLASTIC CLOSING CLAMPS

immediately, but you may still have to manipulate the ribs by pressing in slightly wherever they intrude on the overhang margin. Your can do this by eye, but it's good to check with the caliper as you did on the back. If in spite of every effort the margins don't align absolutely, remain philosophical. Remember we are aiming for excellence, not absolutes. Brush on a little hot water to reflow the glue if necessary and clean up. Remove the alignment pins, if any, so they will not cause problems in the future when the violin has to be opened. Let dry and remove the clamps.

(We have reached a kind of milestone now. The soundbox or "*cassa armonica*" is now complete. We can feel it responding to our voice in sympathetic vibration. We can thump it like a cantaloupe, or spank it like a newborn, hear its response and promise.)

THE SADDLE

Cut the saddle of ebony to a length of 36 mm. Shape the saddle approximately, cut out the purfling and edge to accept it, glue it in, and blend it smoothly into the front channel and edge with knife, file, and scraper. The photo on page 64 shows an overly long (44 mm, but a replacement) saddle. 36 mm is about right, with a level *central* section 18 mm long and concave *side* sections of 9 mm each.

Don't make it a tight fit; this invites cracks at either side when the spruce shrinks more than the ebony.

If there is a hole in the front from an alignment pin, glue in a *shallow* plug now. To avoid difficulty and damage whenever the front has to be removed, it should not extend into the lower block.

MY LABEL IN PLACE FOR POSTERITY

Henry Strobel, Violin Maker
Fecit in Oregon, Anno Domini 1994

GLUING THE FRONT ON

[As with the back, you may decide to first round the edge of the front that goes toward the ribs.]

Gluing the front on is simpler than gluing the back was, since the rib assembly is now stabilized by the back. Use thinner glue, and brush it neatly all around at once. We don't need to preseal the blocks as much as we did for the back, since we want the top to be readily removable.

If the alignment pins are used, everything should fit

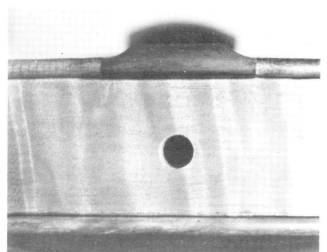

SADDLE INSTALLED, STROBEL (NOTE 1-PIECE RIB)

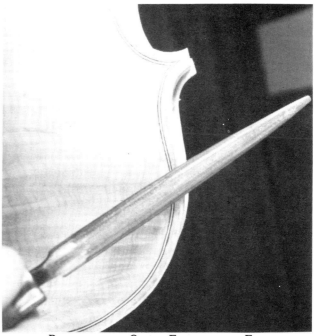

BEVELING THE OUTER EDGE WITH A FILE

THE EDGES

The body is now assembled but the back and front edges are unfinished. We need to properly *round* these. Our fiddle will then suddenly start to look like a violin. (We also need to examine and perhaps retrim the rib ends for the corner overhang of 1.5 to 2 mm.)

See *Art & Method of the Violin Maker*, pages 61-62.

First cut a **bevel** all around the inner edges of back and front with a knife.

[As we noted, This could have been done with a half round file before gluing the back and front on, as many do, but it is easy enough to do now, and leaves a little more freedom in fitting the overhang.]

Repeat this beveling on the outer edge of the front and back with a half round file — flat side on the convex curves, round on the concave.

[A flat-bottomed thumb plane can also be used for bevelling the convex sections of the edge.]

We will now **round** the edge, blending the inner and outer bevels into a smooth curve. This is one of the few places where **sandpaper** is really appropriate on the violin. Coarse sandpaper quickly rounds the edge, and *with reasonable care*, does no harm to the ribs. Greater care is needed at the corners; wrap the sandpaper around a dowel for rounding the adjacent concave sections of the edge. Don't distort or "pinch" the corners. Leave the back button area to be finished after the neck is set.

Now finish the **channel** with a **scraper**, forming a clean crest with the rounded edge. This will give the final personality to your carving.

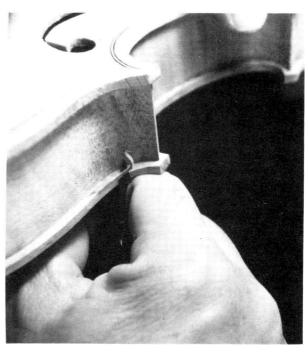

BEVELING THE INNER EDGE WITH A KNIFE

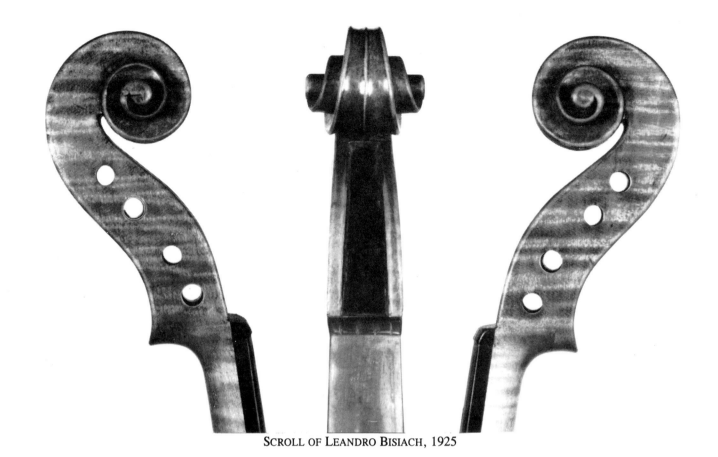

SCROLL OF LEANDRO BISIACH, 1925

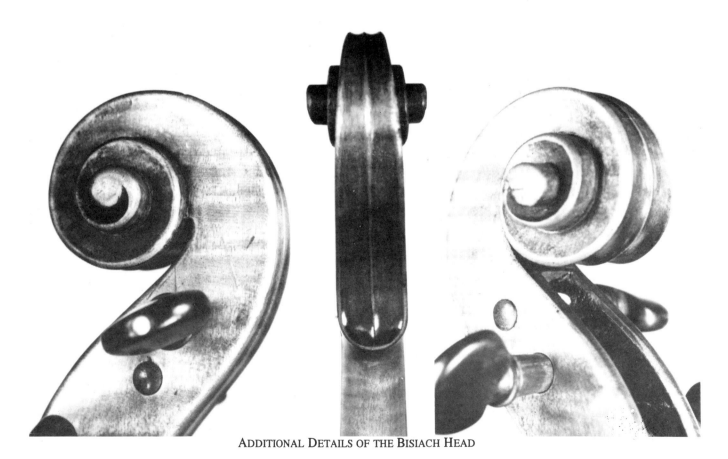

ADDITIONAL DETAILS OF THE BISIACH HEAD

"FORM — The scroll is the maker's hallmark. If regal, the coronation of the violin, if mean, its reproach.

. . . AND FUNCTION" — The neck is the "handle" of the violin, and critical for playability.

Please become familiar with the **Table of Nominal Violin Measurements in Millimeters** on page 43 of this book.

Please also read *Art & Method of the Violin Maker*, page 64-66 for background.

CUTTING IT OUT

Select a piece of **maple**, preferably matching the back and ribs, radially cut, with the outside of the tree toward the fingerboard surface. The wood is usually supplied wedge shaped. Plane the fingerboard surface, then plane both sides *square* to it for an exact width of 42 mm, the width of the scroll. (If the back of the wedge is too narrow for this, glue on temporary pieces of wood.) Use a machine jointer for this if you like.

The neck surface that goes **toward the fingerboard** is now *final*. It should not be necessary to plane it again, since we will **tilt** the fingerboard toward the playing hand by thinning it on the E side.

The tilt of the fingerboard toward the E side is desirable, but not strictly necessary. *See the related note below in the FINGERBOARD section.* Makers have traditionally left the neck surface that goes toward the fingerboard a little high to allow for any needed planing. (We often see a little step, about .5 mm, from this surface down to the pegbox.) The front of the scroll should be about 1 mm back from the plane of this surface, as seen in our scroll profile template. But, as I said, we do not anticipate having to plane this surface again.

Scribe a centerline on it and **lay it out** as in the **full size drawing**, with lines square across to locate upper and lower edges of the **nut** and the **lower end** of the neck, and sloping lines either side of the centerline to locate the **edges** of the fingerboard. Protect this surface with a piece of soft wood or cork whenever it is clamped in the vise.

Make the neck and scroll **profile pattern** of thin sheet aluminum. Clamp this to one side, precisely aligning the nut and fingerboard location. Mark the outline and all the hole centers with a sharp, hard pencil. Repeat on the other side.

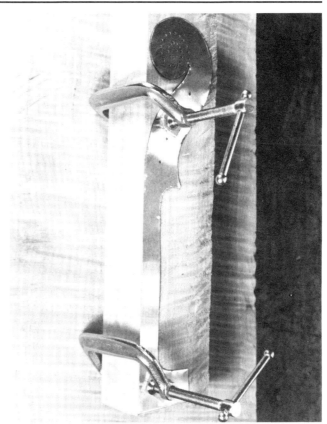

MARKING THE SCROLL PROFILE

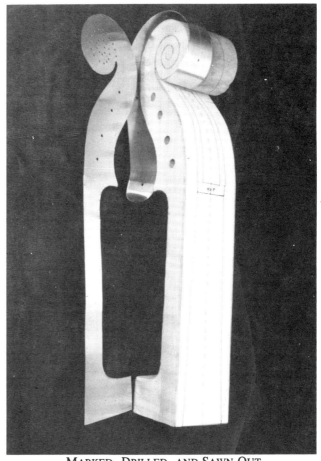

MARKED, DRILLED, AND SAWN OUT

I prefer to drill preliminary peg **holes** now, 5 mm in diameter, with the wood clamped on the drill press table and the drill *precisely* centered on the holes. It's safer to drill halfway through from each side to minimize alignment errors. (The reason for spacing the peg holes in pairs is of course to provide clearance for pegheads and fingers in tuning.)

Saw out the neck and scroll on the **bandsaw**, right up to the line. If you or the saw are prone to wander, leave a little clearance and then finish to the lines on both sides with rasps, files, or sander, etc. Leave the back of the neck and the heel a little full for now. This will be carved to final shape after the neck is mortised into the body. The curved surface of the scroll should be left true and smooth by filing, sanding, or scraping.

The two surfaces at the heel of the neck that go into the mortise must be *flat* and smooth. It is best to finish these on the sander with the table set *square* to the sandpaper. Adjust the fence on the sander table for the correct angle, about 83.5°, at the base of the neck, and then at 90° for the back button surface. But leave a little extra wood on the back button surface until the neck is finally set into the body mortise to adjust it for the right height. Do not remove any wood from the sides yet. This makes it easier to hold in the vise during the next steps.

HOLLOWING THE PEGBOX

There is already a centerline on the fingerboard surface of the neck. Now complete the **centerline** on the front of the pegbox, the front of the volute, over the top of the volute and down the back, using a sharp, hard pencil. If the sides of the neck block were planed parallel and square to the front (fingerboard) surface, you can use a pencil marking gauge. Don't use a knife to scribe this line unless you want it to show in the finished scroll.

Lay out the front opening of the pegbox per the **full size drawing** on page 39, scribing the lines with a knife (or a sharp, hard pencil). A thin flexible steel rule is convenient, or you can make a paper template. Note that the drawing for the front of the pegbox is flat, so it appears longer than the pegbox opening in the side view.

It is helpful to drill some **holes** into the pegbox before chiseling it out. These serve, like the graduating drill, to set the thickness of the back of the pegbox, as well as to remove some of the waste wood, especially if, like me, you are using difficult maple . You can use a dowel set into the drill press table (as we used for preliminary graduation of the back and front) to control the pegbox back thickness to a preliminary 5 or 6 mm,

or you can use a depth stop on your hand drill with the pegbox in the vise. Drill several 6 mm diameter holes on the centerline of the pegbox, nearly merging into a continuous slot.

With the scroll and pegbox held in the vise, cut out the *inside* of the **pegbox** with a **7 mm chisel** for the ends and bottom, and a **14-16 mm chisel** to pare the sides, taking particular care not to chip out at the peg holes. The sides should incline slightly inward so they will be thicker toward the back of the pegbox. We can further refine the inside of the pegbox later; we are roughing it out now while we still have the support of the surrounding wood.

CARVING THE VOLUTE

Of course, like the rest of the violin, we ought perhaps really only need look at a scroll to carve one, but here too a planned methodology helps. We have already established the profile; we now lay out the front and back of the volute, using the **"wraparound" pattern** in the **full size drawings**. Make this pattern of paper or thin metal with inspection holes to line up with the centerline, or of clear, thin plastic with a scribed centerline for alignment.

As in all sculpture we first roughly remove some of the superfluous material before beginning the definitive carving. Place the neck and scroll, fingerboard surface *up*, on the **bandsaw** table. Starting in near the nut, rough saw away the excess wood from the *sides* of the pegbox. Stay well outside the lines to allow for a slight "flare" or widening toward the back and saw right up to the base of the scroll. Back out the bandsaw blade.

[You can now *bandsaw* in from the side at the base of the scroll to release the excess wood from the side of the pegbox. This is the same as cut **1** of the first turn of the volute below; or you can do it with the *backsaw* as described just below.]

Don't saw the excess wood the sides of the fingerboard surface yet. This is kept for now to hold in the vise while we remove excess wood from the volute with the small **backsaw** in the next steps.

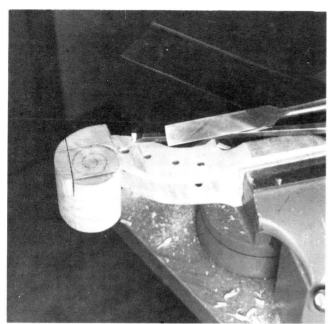

OUTSIDE OF THE PEGBOX AND FIRST VOLUTE CUTS

THE FIRST TURN OF THE VOLUTE — The **first turn** begins at the top of the pegbox. Note the *backsaw cuts* marked **1** through **4** on the **full size scroll profile drawing**. They get successively shorter and shallower as we proceed from the upper side of the pegbox around and outward. With the neck held in the **vise**, make cut **1** (if you have not already done so above on the bandsaw). Next make cut **2**, keeping the saw clear of the layout line going around the scroll. Then *undercut* and remove this piece. Repeat for cuts **3** and **4**. (You can make additional intermediate cuts at 45° to these.) Repeat for the other side of the scroll.

GOUGES — We need several outside beveled **gouges** to properly carve the scroll. These have appropriate **radii** for the purpose (about a no. 7 *"sweep"*), and are available in sets of a dozen or so. For a violin scroll, we can get by with approximate **widths** of 8, 10, 12, 16, and 20 mm. Since a spiral curve has by definition no constant radius, none of these gouges fits *exactly* anywhere, but they are close enough with overlapping cuts. For reference, here is a full size chart of sweeps with various widths, which you can use to identify gouges.

[While the scroll is basically *carved*, at certain steps in certain kinds of fragile, very curly wood (as I am using here) we can use *abrasive* methods to good advantage. Where round or flat **files** or fine **rasps** are indicated, you may prefer to make specialized, more or less permanent tools by gluing **metal backed tungsten carbide** "sandpaper" onto wood. The smooth wood edge lets it be used without damage to an adjacent wall of a volute or bottom of a pegbox.]

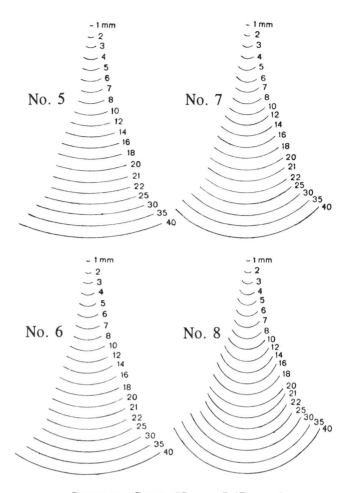

STANDARD GOUGE "SWEEPS" (CURVES)
WITH PERMISSION OF FRANK MITTERMEIER, INC.

High quality "half round" fine **rasps** and **files** are highly recommended, since they actually *cut* rather than just abrade.

We will of course prepare suitably shaped **scrapers** to finish the work after the carving is completed.

Starting with the **larger gouges**, remove the corners left by the saw and *round* the *wall* along the first turn. Also with knife and chisel, *level* and smooth the spiral *face* of the first turn, which is the continuation of the side of the pegbox. Repeat for the other side. Now, viewed from the front, the walls of the first turn should look like a *cylinder* passing straight through the scroll, parallel, with no "undercutting." In fact the walls and faces of the volute are first made completely perpendicular and "flat" before any of the "hollowing" of the faces described below is done.

This is a good time to trim and smooth the bandsawn outer sides of the pegbox to the layout lines with a fine rasp and file. Also round and trim the lower back or "chin" of the scroll with knife and half round file.

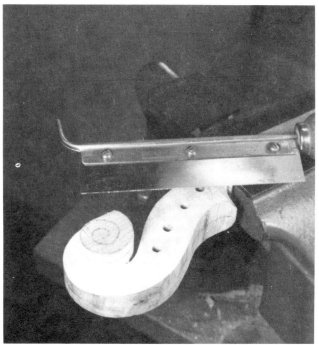

THE FIRST TURN OF THE VOLUTE

THE SECOND TURN OF THE VOLUTE

THE SECOND TURN OF THE VOLUTE — The
second turn is cut in a similar manner, but first we
have to mark it on the *wall* of the first turn, continuing
the line that was left under the volute by the
"wraparound" pattern. Gauge this continuing line about
5 mm out from the *face* of the first turn, proceeding
around to the front of the scroll.

Now use the small backsaw as before to rough out the
second turn, using cuts **5**, **6**, and **7**. Using the **smaller
gouges**, round the wall along the second turn. Also,
with knife and chisel, level and smooth the face of the
second turn, which is the continuation of the first turn.
Repeat on the other side.

Check that the *walls* of this second turn also have the
appearance of a (narrower) cylinder passing through the
scroll. There should be no appearance of hollowing or
undercutting of the walls of the volute. Confirm that the
finished width of the scroll "ear to ear" is 42 mm.

We now have to further continue the outward spiralling
line on the wall of the second turn, after which we can
make cut **8**. You can make one or two additional small
saw cuts if you like, but basically the rest of the
volute's ears are completed *"freehand,"* finishing with
the **smallest gouge**. The ending of the volute spiral in
the ear of the scroll is a prominent characteristic of the
maker's style, so take care here.

THE CHAMFER LINE FOR THE INCURVING —
Now beginning with the *face* at one ear, gauge a
marking line 1 mm in from the edge, continuing along
the second turn, the first turn, down the back side of
the scroll, under and across the "chin," and up the
other side, ending at the other eye of the scroll. Do not
cut *outside* this line, this is reserved for the *chamfer* or
bevel, which will be formed later.

Note: The experienced scroll carver may not actually
draw this chamfer line, nor the chamfer line for the
fluting below. He will visually leave room for the
chamfer as he carves. He may already have been
incurving the face as he progresses, too. But the
instructions here are for the first time carver.

[About now, if the wood is quite soft and prone to chipping
even with the sharpest tools, I may seal it by liberally
brushing on spirit varnish diluted with an equal amount of
alcohol. This soaks in, making the wood stronger and more
uniform after drying, so it can be more smoothly carved and
scraped. Since this solution is the same as my (sparingly
applied) body sealer there is no difference in appearance. It
can be repeated a couple of times during the final carving and
scraping. This is never **necessary**; do it only with "awkward"
wood, not with crisp European maple or pear, nor if it will
interfere with your varnish process.]

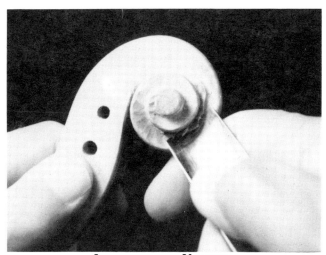

INCURVING THE VOLUTE

INCURVING THE FACES OF THE VOLUTE —
Now **gouge** *inside* the gauged line to incise or "dish" the *face* of the volute, all the while being careful to keep the *walls* of the turns parallel, not undercut. This is done with a sequence of two different **gouge cuts**: The *first cuts* are in and down from the chamfer line toward the wall. The *second cuts* are straight down along the wall, releasing the chips that were raised by the first cuts. For these second, vertical cuts the sweep gouge should match the curvature of the wall. The scroll is now beginning to look like one, at least on the sides. Compare the sides and refine them. **Scrape** the faces and walls smooth, crisp and clean. Satisfy your eye and good taste.

Before going on to the fluting, be sure that the width of the volute is correct everywhere, especially in the front. After fluting it cannot be reduced without distorting the profile.

THE CHAMFER LINE FOR THE FLUTING — We still have to carve the two **grooves** or *fluting* on the back, top, and front of the volute. First gauge another line (much as we did above on the faces or sides of the scroll). This time begin with the *wall* of the eye, 1 mm in from the edge, continuing along the turns, down the back of the scroll, across and up, ending at the other eye. Don't cut the chamfer yet.

FLUTING THE SCROLL — Working inside the chamfer line, and preserving the centerline, carve the concave grooves with gouge and knife (and perhaps a round file over the top), finishing with a curved scraper.

MAKING THE CHAMFER — With a file, followed by a scraper, bevel the edge by cutting at 45° between the gauged lines. Since these are each 1 mm from the edge, the chamfer should be about 1.4 mm wide. This will

vary with your style. A wide chamfer gives an impression of more mass, a narrow one of fragility.

Note: It is essential for the beginner to have a good scroll of the desired model at hand to study as he carves. But beware (or be aware) if it is a machine carved one. These are often of a good model, but lack crispness and individuality. They may have tapered "flowerpot" ears, "fillets" where the walls and faces of the volute meet, and perhaps even obvious regular tool marks, all depending on the limitations of the carving machine. Do not copy these characteristics in your scroll!

NARROW THE NECK — The fingerboard surface of the neck was left wide for handling in the vise, but now we have to cut off the excess wood outside the lines that locate the sides of the fingerboard. Place the neck, fingerboard surface up, on the bandsaw table and saw just outside the lines.

The lower end of the neck has already been accurately cut for the angles of the mortise and back button, but we still need to cut off the extra wood along the sides of the bottom of the neck to fit the sloping sides of the mortise. If you have not already done so, lay out these sloping lines on the *base* of the neck. See the **full size drawings**. Trim to these lines with rasp and block plane or scraper.

[An easier way to trim to these lines, especially in highly figured wood is on the sander. Set the fence and guide for this compound cut, which follows both the sloping lines on the base of the neck and the edges of the fingerboard surface of the neck. But only use the sander for this if you can use it accurately. Power tools can quickly get out of control, rounding and ruining otherwise fine work. Learn to do such jobs *by hand first*, and you may not want to use power.]

THE FINGERBOARD

See the **full size drawings** for the fingerboard **radius gauge**. You may want to make one from thin wood or aluminum.

Buy a **first quality ebony** fingerboard. It should come with the correct **radius** of curvature, 42 mm. (Note that this is radius is approximate. Ideally the radius is *slightly less* toward the G side and *slightly more* toward the E side and at the nut.

It should also have a slight **longitudinal concavity** (0.5 mm under the E string, 0.7 mm under the G). Check this with a steel rule laid edgewise on the fingerboard. This lengthwise hollowing is to provide clearance for the vibrating string. If not, correct this with a small **block plane**, extremely sharp and set for a very thin cut, and scraper, followed by 320, then 600 grit wet sandpaper on a block. While the ebony dust slurry is still wet, rub the fingerboard vigorously with a paper towel until dry to polish it. (The same process will be used years later to remove the furrows of playing, a reason not to make the fingerboard too thin at first.)

The fingerboard top surface can be planed by working against a low bench stop, but it is better to make a tapered holding fixture by gluing two thin strips of wood to a board, which is then clamped to the bench. (If it is planed on the violin, remove the nut first, place a shield under the fingerboard to protect the varnish of the front, and take care not to nick the scroll.)

The fingerboard is still oversize. Mark the width on the underside and **narrow** it to fit the neck, leaving the final scraping for later. It is still too thick; **thin it** by planing the *underside*. Check with rule and surface plate to make sure this is *flat*, not twisted or rounded.

[Instead of planing I prefer to do this on the flat table of the belt **sander**. This is fairly safe and controlled. *A machine jointer in this case is not!*]

The edges should be initially about 5.5 mm thick on the G side, about 0.7 mm thinner on the E side.

This is for a slight tilt toward the playing hand. It should not be overdone; the common practice of planing the neck surface itself to get this tilt is not really necessary. (The tilt is reversed on the cello and bass, both for comfort and to give bow clearance at the treble side, especially on wide models. There the top of the neck may be planed slightly downward to the bass side.)

The fingerboard is also probably just slightly too long. Using the table and guide of the disk sander, **square** and trim the ends, leaving it 270 mm long.

The part of the fingerboard projecting beyond the neck is still too heavy. Place the fingerboard upside down with the wide end against a wood stop. Beginning from

THE LOWER END OF MY FINGERBOARD

the lower end of the neck gradually **hollow** the underside with gouge and scraper, tapering to a thickness of about 3.5 mm at the lower end. But keep this hollowing at least 1.5 mm away from the edges of the board, which are left about 5 mm high for rigidity.

[It is optional to gouge a shallow central groove about 6 mm wide on the underside of the fingerboard where it glues to the neck. This makes gluing and removal easier, and reduces its weight a little. Do *not* groove the neck itself.]

The fingerboard is always removably glued to the neck with thin hot glue, but now **glue it on** *very* lightly for setup and testing, since we will remove it soon for varnishing.

A nicety often neglected is the subtle concavity along the *sides* of the fingerboard. This agrees with and complements the longitudinal concavity on the *top* of the fingerboard. It is only about 0.5 mm on each side at the middle of the string length. It results in a slight flare toward the lower end, but don't cut into the *neck* to get this non essential nicety. (After the fingerboard has been replaced several times, this will doubtless occur anyway!)

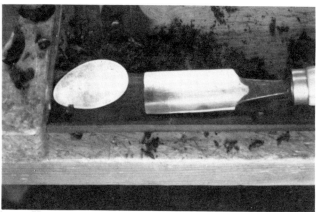

HOLLOWING THE FINGERBOARD UNDERNEATH

FINGERBOARD RADIUS AND NUT TEMPLATE

THE NUT

This is of course of ebony with the grain across the neck. On many violins, as on this one, it widens upward to the pegbox. Its shape can be seen in the photos; its size and grooves are given in the **table**. Hold it in place and scribe it at the sides of the pegbox and, for now, about 2 mm above the fingerboard.

Saw and shape it approximately (the sander is convenient) and glue it to the top of the fingerboard. (It will be temporarily removed with the fingerboard for varnishing.) It is now fitted in place, the ends perfectly flush with the fingerboard and sides of the pegbox, rounded at the top, with no sharp edges. The top of the nut should be about 1 mm over the fingerboard, smoothly rounded down toward and merging into the slope of the pegbox. Use a file, followed by fine sandpaper. (See *Useful Measurements for Violin Makers*, page 20.)

The centers of the E and G strings are about 16.4 mm apart, and shifted about 0.5 mm toward the G side. Locate the centers of the A and D strings with dividers, or use the template in the **full size drawings** to mark the groove centers with a knife.

Nut files with smooth sides are available to form these grooves to a definite width. You can also use a triangular file to *start* the grooves, but always end up with a "**mouse tail**" **file** to smooth the grooves and round them over down toward the pegbox. The *highest* part of the groove should be at the start of the fingerboard. See the **table of measurements** for string *spacing* and *clearance*, which should never be less than the thickness of a stiff business card.

Lubricate the grooves with graphite from the point of a pencil.

ATTACHING THE NECK

Lay out the **mortise** on the upper **ribs** and the upper **front** in light pencil. You can use the template for the lower end of the neck given in the **full size drawings**. These are *approximate* guide lines only. The final cuts are determined during the fitting of the neck (with the

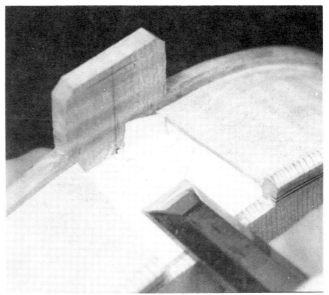

CUTTING THE NECK MORTISE

fingerboard attached), for the correct alignment and elevation. The mortise is gradually cut with a **chisel**, working from the middle out.

Patience and precision are needed as we repeatedly test and pare until the neck can just be pushed into a *perfect, tight fit,* with the following conditions met:

1 — The **fingerboard** is centered over the front centerline.

2 — The **neck** and scroll are vertical (not twisted sideways.)

3 — The **nut** is 130 mm from the upper front edge.

4 — The **depth** of the mortise lets the lower end of the neck extend to the inner edge of the purfling groove or a little past it.

5 — The **height** of the fingerboard over the upper edge of the front is 6 to 6.5 mm.

6 — The **projection** of the fingerboard at the bridge line is 27 mm.

7 — The **heel** of the neck meets the back button tightly all around and is sufficient for the back button height of 13 mm.

The neck, with the fingerboard still temporarily glued on, is glued and clamped exactly into the mortise as shown by the *lower* clamp (only) in the photo on page 77. Use strong, hot glue and clean up with hot water.

Study the STANDARD VIOLIN DIAGRAM on page 22 of *Useful Measurements for Violin Makers*.

You might want to make an **L-shaped gauge** of 3 mm thick wood to check this important *27 mm fingerboard projection*. It also checks the neck length, fingerboard length, and bridge location. See the **full size drawing** on page 40.

[Or, you can simply place one rule on the fingerboard and check the elevation at the bridge line with another, as I do.]

FINISHING THE NECK

See the **full size drawings** on page 40 for a **neck template**; make this in thin metal or rib stock. The back and base of the neck are still "square" and the back button oversize. These are now rounded and reduced to the final shape with knife, **half round and flat rasps and files**, **scraper** and **fine sandpaper**.

Using the neck template, test for the correct neck *thickness* and the upper and lower *cross sections*, and for the desired *radii* at the scroll and heel of the neck. A common mistake of the beginner is to make the heel too bulky. Study these curves from all directions in light and shadow. Make them as smooth and artistic as you can. Some practice and skill is needed to manipulate the file to avoid flat spots and make the curves flow *smoothly*. Blend the neck smoothly into the bottom side of the fingerboard. Some have a better eye for this than others. Be sure to feel these curves too to detect "bumps". Study the photos of the back of the

scroll (at the beginning of this chapter) and the back button (below).

A standard test is to measure with **dividers** from where the edge of the front joins the side of the neck to the centerline of the heel. This is typically 26 mm.

Sand the neck with 150 grit paper. Wrap it around your finger for the upper and lower neck curves. Follow with 220 and 400.

Note that the **chin** of the scroll rises *higher* than typical on the Bisiach. Ordinarily it is about level with the lower edge of the nut to form a point of reference for the first position. See the template on the **full size drawings**.

Note too that the **back button** is a little *wider* than typical on our Bisiach, a little over 22 mm. I have given the more typical figure of 21 in the **table**. Follow these stylistic variations if you like.

Now that the neck is complete, so is the fingerboard, except for its sides. They are not vertically flat, but are merged smoothly into the more or less elliptical or parabolic curve of the neck section. This is true for about the lower 2/3 of the fingerboard sides. We then

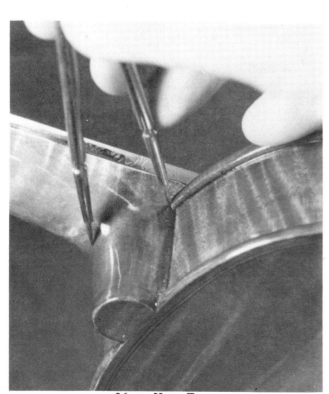

26 MM HEEL TEST

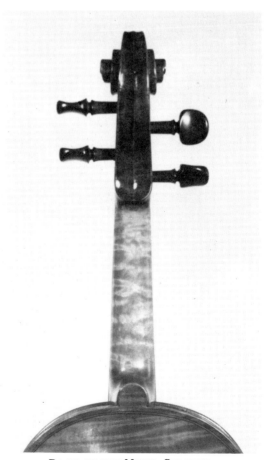

BACK OF THE NECK, STROBEL

scrape about a mm wide (no more) chamfer on the top edges of the fingerboard sides. The upper edge of this chamfer is smoothed with fine sandpaper, and its lower edge is merged with the upper 1/3 of the side of the fingerboard. There must be no sharp edges on the fingerboard and on the nut, which would be bothersome in playing. (But don't carry this rounding too far into the playing surface of the fingerboard, which would make stopping the E string insecure.)

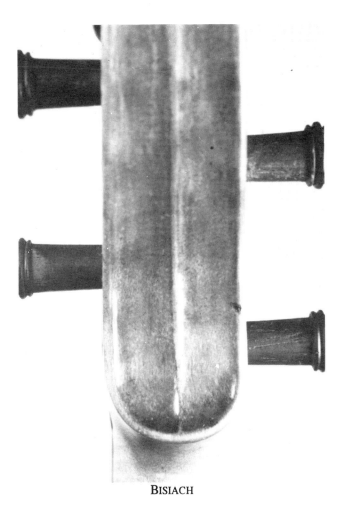

BISIACH

COMPOUND CURVES OF THE (GRAFTED) NECK, BISIACH

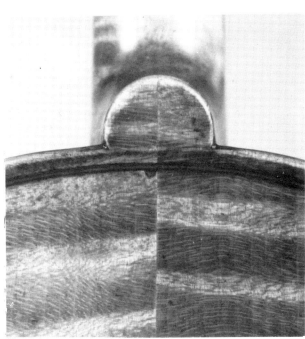

BACK BUTTON, BISIACH

We will be fairly thorough in this chapter, since it is so important to the tone and playability of the violin. You will also find this information useful in setting up other violins. The techniques shown are chosen for both accuracy and efficiency.

The violin will be supported in a cloth or carpet lined bench cradle during these operations, except when it is held, violin maker style, between the knees.

Please read *Art & Method of the Violin Maker*, pages 62, 73-76, and *Useful Measurements for Violin Makers*, pages 19-23. Refer also to the TABLE in this book.

We will *fit up* the violin and **test** it before varnishing. We are naturally eager to hear it, but want to avoid rushing the varnish.

It is also important to be sure that everything fits for good **playability**, and there is nothing wrong with the **tone** that cannot be taken care of with varnish and adjustment. Most violins seem to sound loud, very responsive, and a little less refined "in the white."

In most cases we will not actually *make* the fittings, but buy them ready made (oversize) and *fit* them to our violin.

THE PEGS
_____

See *Art & Method of the Violin Maker*, pages 73-74.

Check the *preliminary* peg holes for correct layout. If necessary you can shift them a little with a round file before reaming, or by manipulating the **reamer** to the

REAMING THE PEG HOLES

side while reaming. Look at the reamer from the front and top to check that you are reaming the hole straight across. They should finish with at least 2 mm **clearance** at the back of the pegbox, and with minimal, if any, rubbing of the A string over the D peg.

The **reamer** will have a taper of 1:30, 5.5 to 10 mm in diameter. (A smaller one, 4 to 7.5 mm is good for starting the holes and, of course, for small instruments.)

A simple, versatile tool is a hardwood **peg holding block** with a range of tapered holes. This is held in the bench vise. Insert the peg and turn it while scoring it with a knife at the collar. This prevents the collar from chipping in the shaper.

A little **beeswax** rubbed on the peg will help it turn smoothly in the shaper. Shape the peg right up to the collar. If your shaper is working *correctly*, you should

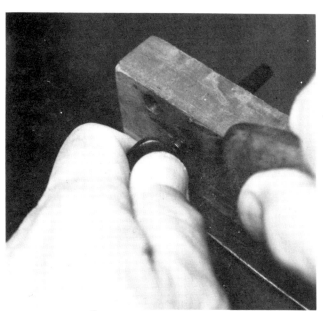

SCORING AT THE COLLAR

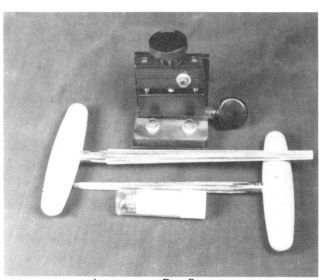

ADJUSTABLE PEG SHAPER,
REAMERS, AND PEG COMPOUND

SHAPING THE PEG
(I MADE THIS OLD TOOL OF WALNUT WOOD.)

FILING THE STRING HOLE AFTER DRILLING

Mark the peg with a pencil in the *middle* of the pegbox for the **string hole**. (Or the hole can be a little closer to

not need to further sand or polish the peg. After shaping apply **peg compound** liberally, and firmly turn the peg into the hole.

DRILLING THE STRING HOLE

SAWING THE PEG TO LENGTH

ROUNDING THE PEG END

ENDBUTTON ON THE BISIACH

the peg head to allow for the peg's drifting farther into the pegbox with wear.)

Also mark the peg with a knife just outside the pegbox for length. Saw the peg to length in the holding block with a small **backsaw**, while rotating the peg toward the saw to prevent splitting off. Place the peg in the holding block, drill a clean 1.4 mm **string hole** and "chamfer" it with a small round file.

Now finish the peg ends to a suitable radius by rotating and rubbing on sandpaper (medium, then fine) in the hollow of a long gouge. The edge of the end will be crisp, not "rounded." I finish with 600 paper followed by a brisk rub on canvas (my shop apron) to polish.

THE ENDBUTTON

See the photo. The **endbutton** is nominally centered on the rib joint, but there are logical structural reasons for placing it a *little* below center, and also angled *slightly* down. The strings will tend to pull it into the perpendicular, not out of it, and will thus not place stress on the collar of the endbutton.) The hole is made with the peg **reamer**. As with the pegs, it is better to reduce the diameter of the endbutton rather than ream out the hole to fit an oversize one.

THE POST

One hears opinions about the diameter and hardness of the post and its effect on **tone**, but the most important things are its **position** relative to the bridge, and its **tightness** front to back. Select a 6 mm post with closely spaced annual rings. Measure the approximate **length** required with a sound post length **gauge** at the usual post position.

With a *sharp* knife cut the post to length, a little oversize at first, visually fitting the **ends** to the curvature of the arching. Stick the sharpened end of an S-shaped post **setter** into the right (short) side of the post, about a third of the way down from the top. The **annual rings** in the post of course run *across* those in the front. Insert the post through the *right* soundhole

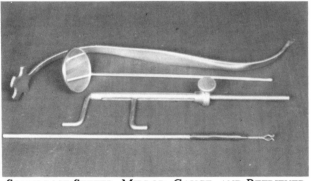

SOUNDPOST SETTER, MIRROR, GAUGE, AND RETRIEVER

and set it into its approximate position, looking through the endbutton hole and right sound hole to see that it is *vertical* crosswise and lengthwise .

It will likely take several trials to get the length and fit perfect, as indeed it must be. The bevel on the ends must be correct and flat. No rounded or splintered edges, please. Check the fit to the arching by looking through the endbutton hole. An inspection **mirror** and small **light** used through the soundhole are helpful. The ends of the post are finally fitted with a fine **file**, then slightly moistened before placing. See *Useful Measurements for Violin Makers*, page 23, to measure the post position with a **business card gauge**.

Of course we do not yet have the bridge but we can set the post approximately. The edge of the post is typically 3 mm from that of the bridge (lengthwise of the violin), farther if the front is thick, closer if thin. If necessary, move it toward the bridge to brighten the tone or to help even out "rough" spots around B or C. Crosswise of the violin the post is about 1 mm inside the right foot of the bridge. Too tight a post can "choke" the lower register; free it up by a slight movement toward the bar. Tightness may vary with seasonal changes.

Never make the post too tight. This invites a disastrous crack and distorts the body. It should just slip into place without string tension. Run your fingertip over the upper wing of the right soundhole. If it is high the post is probably too tight.

THE STRINGS

See *Useful Measurements for Violin Makers*, pages 19-21.

Select a set of high quality strings. The most practical and generally satisfactory type are the wound multi-filament synthetics (silver G, aluminum D and A), although you may prefer the more traditional wound gut strings, with possibly a plain A. The E string is always steel, usually plain. The aluminum wound E's are rather fragile but may have some playing advantages. There is usually no reason to use other than the *medium* gauge.

The A, D, G string ends are simply held in the notches of the tailpiece. They are *not* threaded through their loop ends.

The end of the string extends through the hole in the peg about 6 mm. Take one turn over this end to lock it, then wind the rest in a single layer, ending just *at* the wall of the pegbox, *not* tight against it. This retains the peg in the hole, without damaging the string or the pegbox, or making the peg hard to turn.

PEGS AND STRINGS ON THE BISIACH

Note: Do not actually install the strings until after the bridge feet have been fitted as described on page 67.

THE TAILPIECE

Select a matching **tailpiece**, preferably of the *Hill* style, and fit it with a smoothly working E string **tuner** and a black nylon **"tailgut"** with threaded brass adjusting nuts. Set these so the lower end of the tailpiece is just even with the outside edge of the saddle when the strings are tight. Trim off any excess length. Set the tailpiece aside until it is needed to test the string clearance of the bridge.

THE BRIDGE

See *Useful Measurements for Violin Makers*, pages 21-22. Also see *Art & Method of the Violin Maker*, pages 74-75.

The post should be in place before fitting the bridge.

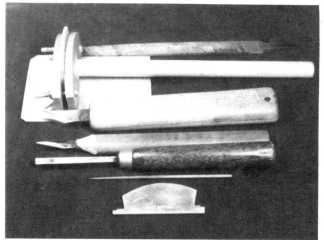

BRIDGE FITTING TOOLS
(FILE, HOLDER, SANDPAPER, FOOT & ARCH KNIFE,
OPENING KNIFE, CHISEL, GROOVE FILE, TEMPLATE)

THE BRIDGE BLANK AND ORIENTATION — Use the highest quality only, such as the French deluxe "treated" ones. These are hard, fine grained, and have a nice tan color. Examine the wood of the bridge. You will see that one side, usually that with the manufacturer's stamp, is exactly cut on the quarter, and shows the **long rays**. This side is left essentially as is and faces the *tailpiece*. The other side is thus slightly off the quarter cut, and shows the short sectioned rays or **"spots."** Nearly all the thinning and tapering is done on this side, which faces the *fingerboard*. After the bridge is completed and tested, I stamp my name (if it's a good violin) on this side.

[Some prefer to place the long rays toward the fingerboard; that's OK, too.]

See *Useful Measurements for Violin Makers*, page 22, for the STANDARD VIOLIN DIAGRAM.

Look at the bridge from the side of the violin. Note that it appears to be tilting back toward the tailpiece. This is approximately the same as having the back side of the bridge vertical, or at a right angle to the plane of the ribs. The centerline of the bridge should *bisect* the angle of the string over the bridge for equilibrium (stability).

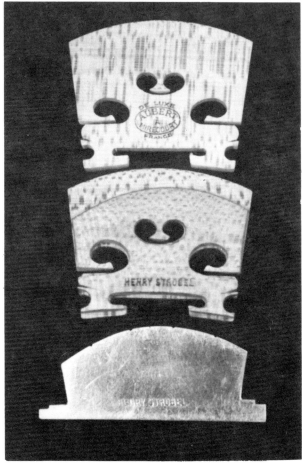

BRIDGE BACK, FRONT, FITTED, AND TEMPLATE

Don't worry about the actual string angle. This will be OK if the other measurements are. (In Useful Measurements for Violin Makers I suggested using a gauge to check this, but I rarely do.)

Periodically check the bridge for the correct angle, especially after changing strings. Tuning pulls the top of the bridge toward the pegs, eventually warping it, keeping it from resting flat on the soundboard. This is

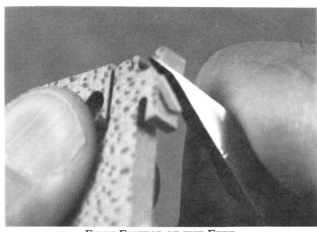

FIRST FITTING OF THE FEET

bad for tone, and also somewhat similar to moving the post back away from the bridge.

Make a **bridge template** like that in the photo. Select a high quality unfitted bridge. The "before and after" photos show typical changes that may be made in fitting it. These are described in detail below.

TRIMMING THE FEET — We will remove wood from the *bottom* of the feet to leave them 1 mm high and fitting the front surface of the violin. (This fit is easily achieved on our new violin, but might be much more complicated on an old one dented by previous bridges.) Cut this wood away by eye with a **knife**, allowing for the *vertical* orientation of the backside of the bridge. This can be done *approximately*, since we will fit the feet with the **bridge sanding fixture** below.

SANDING THE FEET TO FIT — It is simple to make a fixture similar to the one in the photographs. The back side of the bridge must be vertical when centered on the line connecting the two inner soundhole notches. Medium sandpaper, followed by fine, is held face up with one hand while the other rubs the bridge, with about a 10 mm stroke, along the centerline of the front of the violin. The fitting of the feet will be finished with the **curved scraper** later.

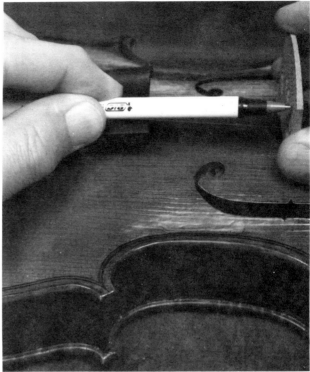

PRELIMINARY MARKING OF THE BRIDGE HEIGHT

MARKING THE BRIDGE HEIGHT — Hold the bridge in place and mark the fingerboard side with an *8 mm diameter ball point pen* laid flat on the fingerboard at the positions of the E and G strings. The mark at the E string location is about right, but make a new mark 2 mm higher at the G string location. Use these marks to locate the bridge template and trace the bridge top arching onto the bridge.

More elegant bridge **height marking gauges** can readily be devised, but it is basically a trial and error process, and the actual height will be determined by the **string clearance gauges** on the sides of the **bridge template**. The higher steps of the clearance gauges are nominally for gut, the lower for steel core strings.

The steel **E clearance** at the end of the fingerboard may vary from 2.5 to 3.5 mm, depending on player preference, assuming a normal fingerboard longitudinal concavity.

The **G clearance** at the end of the fingerboard will be about 5.5 mm for gut, 5.0 for synthetic, and 4.0 for steel core strings.

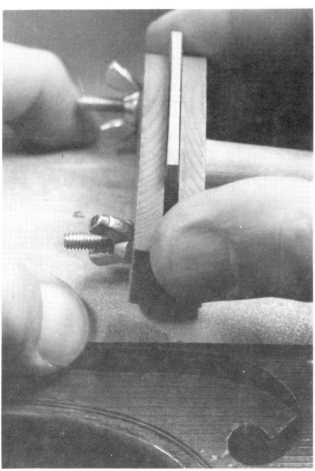

SANDING THE FEET TO FIT THE FRONT

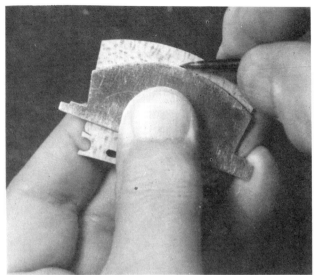

TRACING THE TOP ARCH

FORMING THE BRIDGE TOP — Trim the top of the bridge to the arching line (or not quite to it for a conservative first trial) with a knife and file.

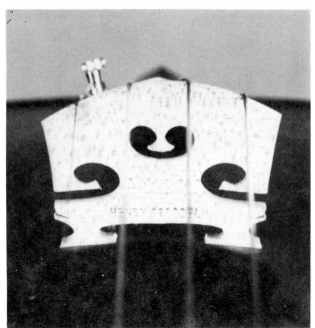

THE BRIDGE OVER THE BISIACH

[Or on the disk sander if you're impatient.]

Using the template as a guide, file very shallow grooves for the strings. These should be shifted a little toward the bass side, leaving a little more space to the outside of the E string because of the greater slope there.

[Of course you can use dividers instead of the template to locate the string grooves. Space the E and G strings 33.5 mm center to center and divide the path along the top arch into three equal lengths.]

Now place the bridge in position on the violin and install first the E, then the G string. Check the string clearance and correct it if necessary. Use a **bridge jack** or a used bridge to temporarily support the strings while you remove the new bridge. Place the jack right up against the bridge to provide an exact reference position when later placing the bridge back on the violin.

THINNING THE BRIDGE — Thinning removes excess wood from the front (fingerboard side) of the bridge. Traditionally done with **chisel** and **plane**, this is more easily and faster done on the bench **belt sander**. (Watch out for your fingertips!)

Refine the front surface on a **fine sanding board**, followed optionally by a **fine file**. (An ordinary office clipboard makes a convenient sanding board; it can hold several sheets of sandpaper of varying grits.) The bridge will have a finished thickness of about 4.3 mm at the feet and 1.3 mm along the entire arched top. This will result in a slightly convex front face, about 4 mm thick in the middle. The back (tailpiece side) of the bridge is left *flat*.

[However, many makers do a little of the thinning on the back, with the *top* part of the back *very* slightly convex tapered.]

With a convex edged **scraper**, make the feet of the bridge very slightly hollow. This will help them to fit tightly all around under pressure from the strings. This tight fit is important for tone.

COMPLETING THE BRIDGE — At this point we have a *plain bridge* that fits the violin and will work, but we now proceed to complete the acoustic and artistic touches that will give a *"professionally fitted"* **look** and, we hope, **sound** to our bridge. Cutting a bridge is personal and artistic; this is an *example*.

As for **tone**, three things are significant, given a standard pattern (as the *Aubert*):

1 — The **wood**, its density, stiffness, and damping.

2 — The general **thickness** of the bridge. You may want to try different thicknesses to note the effect on tone. (The height is determined by our standard fingerboard projection.)

3 — How we **"cut"** the bridge, or *modify the pattern*, is the subject of this section. All these cuts are a matter of degree, according to the insights and habits of the violin maker. There is definitely more art than science to this. I can't explain (without rationalizing) how all these variables work together, but will show how I cut

a typical bridge anyway. In general, cutting away wood reduces stiffness more significantly than mass, so the net effect of cutouts is to lower the vibration frequencies of the bridge, reducing unpleasant higher frequency sounds. But we can't go too far or the tone will suffer and the bridge will look uncouth.

You might wonder why the bridge manufacturer doesn't do some of this for us. To some extent the violin maker knows how to optimize the standard bridge for a particular violin. And different violins do require different bridges. Also — a well cut bridge is a minor work of art, a signature of and perhaps an advertisement for the maker.

FINISHING THE BRIDGE — *Although we used sandpaper to thin and smooth the face of the bridge, we have no further use for it on the bridge. The rest of the cutting is done with knife or chisel with crisp, clean, graceful cuts. The cuts are flat along the width, never rounded or sloped. (A fine sharp file is used only at the top of the bridge.)*

The results of most of the **15 steps** below can be seen in the fitted bridges shown on pages 66 and 68. A variety of anatomical terms have been applied to the bridge; I hope mine have not added to the confusion.

1 — Smooth the **top edge** flat with a file. Then file a narrow 45° bevel (chamfer) on its front and back. Further chamfer the upper edges of each of these two chamfers (at the top of the bridge). Other than this chamfering do not further thin the top. There should be no sharp edge, especially at the back where the string goes down toward the tailpiece.

2 — Refine the **string grooves** with the mouse tail file, rounding them slightly downward at the back where the strings slope downward toward the tailpiece. The grooves are relatively *shallow* and wide, so the strings rest "on" rather than "in" them. The depth of these grooves is *nominally* 1/3 the string diameter, and they are just wide enough not to pinch the strings, which must slide smoothly across as it is tuned up to pitch.

3 — Finish and **chamfer** the upper sides, both front and back, with a knife (or *maybe* a file). First take a very light cut off the face of the sides to remove any tool marks. It's OK if this makes the side *very slightly* concave, but they are usually straight. Now cut the chamfers with the knife upward, narrowing them a little as you go toward the top. The back chamfer can be somewhat narrower than the front one.

4 — Raise the **under arch** with the knife. Not too much, but enough to at least match its curve to that of the violin and not appear flat or squat. You *can* use a

round file at the inside of the feet, but a narrow knife should suffice.

5 — Trim the **feet** to a level height of 1 mm, cutting with the knife at right angles to the back of the bridge for a level height. Bevel the inside and outside ends of the feet with knife or chisel. The feet will be about 11.5 mm long, maintaining an overall width at the feet of 41 mm.

6 — Trim the outside curves just above the feet to within about 0.5 mm of the **"bee stings."**

7 — Enlarge the lower curve of the **"heart,"** taking care not to damage the small internal points.

8 — Enlarge the **"eyes"** but don't go closer to the heart than about 5 mm. Enlarging the eyes up and outward mainly removes mass, but enlarging toward the heart decreases stiffness. Keep the eyes at least 15.5 mm apart at the **"waist."**

9 — Thin the **"legs"** and lower the **"knees"** with a knife. Make sure the top of the leg slopes downward to the outside, and don't make the leg thinner than about 5 mm.

10 — Taper the **points** (at the bottom of the "eyes"), front and back with a small chisel, primarily to keep them from catching the wiping cloth.

11 — Emphasize the **"bee stings"** with a knife. This looks nice, and of course also affects the tuning of the bridge.

12 — You may give the finished bridge —*except* the feet — a coat of *thin* spirit **varnish**. Let dry. It's perfectly OK to omit this step, as I often do.

[Some "condition" bridges in ammonia fumes, apply linseed oil, bake or microwave them, etc. To each his own.]

13 — Glue a pad of thin, nearly transparent **parchment** (about 4 mm by 10 mm and .15 mm thick) over the E groove. This keeps the steel string from cutting into the wood. It also acts as a minor high frequency "tone filter." Moisten it, fold and glue it over the groove, indent it with a fingernail, and hold it until the glue grabs.

14— Lubricate the grooves with **graphite** from a pencil point.

15 — **Stamp** your name over the under arch using your hardened steel stamp. I simply ink it on a stamp pad and strike it lightly with the purfling hammer.

[Others may use lampblack, or actually burn it on with heat.]

TESTING

Set up the bridge, add the D, then A strings, and tune
to pitch, pulling the bridge back to its right angle as the
strings stretch. Install a **chinrest** of your choice. The
chin rest is important. It will help prevent soiling the
white wood; it will also allow the front to vibrate freely
to assess the tone.

This is usually a time of relief, maybe rejoicing. Let's
not be too hasty or critical at this moment. The tone
will likely improve with varnish and further adjustment,
and perhaps with settling and playing, too. Only if there
is something clearly wrong should we consider altering
the bar or graduation at this point.

(The violin I am making has a *lot* of sound, and a free,
full lower register, which I have come to expect with
this deeply curled, *very flexible* maple wood! I don't
think stiffness is desirable everywhere, especially in the
ribs. The D is already beautiful. The A is clear and
even, but it and the E are a little aggressive. I withhold
any judgment since the varnish will have a damping
effect. Also I have been hasty in trying the violin and
the neck still needs to be thinned and smoothed, which
will have an effect, too.)

So let's enjoy it for a bit, try a few exploratory post
adjustments, and proceed to remove the fingerboard and
fittings in preparation for varnishing.

BEFORE STARTING

First, we need to understand that the varnish, unless used in excess, is much more important *æsthetically* than *acoustically*. The varnish is what one sees first of all, and everyone notices color, whether or not they appreciate the style of model and carving. How a violin is varnished determines *first its appearance*, next its *surface durability*, but only *last its tone*.

If the varnish is poor, the violin will be rejected before a bow touches it. Yes, "It's the tone that matters," but there are plenty of good sounding violins that look good too.

While bad varnish can ruin a violin, good varnish gives us a great opportunity for personal artistic style. A huge range of color, material, texture, shading. and transparency is available. Good varnishing is not easy, and mastery does not come without difficulty, discipline, and experience.

Varnish is often described as *oil* or *spirit*, as we will below, but we should not generalize too much about their characteristics. Either kind can be good or bad, and very often both are used on the same violin in different coats, along with *water* stains, etc.

Refer also to *Art & Method of the Violin Maker*, pages 71-72 and *Violin Maker's Notebook*, pages 31-39.

SURFACE PREPARATION — Remove all the fittings and the fingerboard, which was glued on lightly with this in mind. Lightly glue a fitted shield of wood or strong cardboard to the fingerboard mounting surface of the neck for protection from handling and varnish.

Inspect the surface overall for imperfections in finish, dents, and dirt. Remove any remaining glue spots with water and a stiff brush. Scrutinize and **refine** if necessary the neck curves. Do any light last minute scraping you see indicated. Swell out any dents with locally applied hot water. Do not ruin crisp edges with sandpaper, although a little fine sandpaper clean up of ribs, neck, and smooth areas of the back is OK, depending on the kind of finish we want. I think a *smoothly scraped* surface is always desirable. It is particularly important for the *front* surface to be nicely scraped, with the grain.

Now is the time to moisten the wood overall with a wet **sponge**. This will raise the grain (unless you have previously sealed it in places) and give an attractive texture. Let it dry completely. Some like to sand this off and repeat for a flat finish; we, however, appreciate this natural look, and will not. What we will do is rub

the dried surface briskly with the synthetic mesh pad mentioned below to get a smooth "satin" surface.

(See also the note on *rubbing* on page 49 under THE LABEL.)

Fit a tapered **dowel** snugly into the endbutton hole. This will serve as a handle or rest during varnishing. It can also be clamped into a vise for support while drying.

Literally any number of materials, combinations, and methods could be (and have been) used with good and bad results.

The procedure described below will probably give an acceptable result for the beginner, and was chosen with that in mind. It is not necessarily the easiest, and certainly not the fastest way. Varnishing remains a personal, problematic, process. I will also assume here that we are buying, not making our varnish. That would be a subject for another — someone else's — book.

SOME MATERIALS FOR VARNISHING

SPIRIT VARNISH — **Spirit varnish** dries *rapidly* by the evaporation of the volatile solvent. It is thus more difficult to apply smoothly with a brush. It also tends to redissolve the previous coat, so we cannot brush back over the freshly applied varnish to level it. Use a wide brush, full of varnish. You may be able to lessen the brushing problem by adding a small amount of slower drying essential (evaporating) oil such as **lavender** or **rosemary** to retard drying. Add a little at a time and test it first. With numerous thin color coats, the inevitable unevenness of the individual coats will average out.

[Or completely eliminate the problem by spraying it with an **air brush**. In spraying spirit varnish, one can put essentially all the color "coats" on in one session. Level any "orange peel" on the surface by wet sanding the still thick and tender varnish the next day. Watch out for fingerprints, etc. French polish it. In a few weeks the varnish will have hardened and shrunk down onto the wood like a thin skin. There are indeed many ways to varnish.]

OIL VARNISH — **Oil varnish** dries partly by evaporation of its thinner, spirits of turpentine, for example, but primarily by the hardening of the non-evaporating oil component such as linseed. It thus "dries" *slowly* and tends to level itself, making brushing easier, but requiring more time before it can be recoated or rubbed. Some oil varnishes require sunlight (or ultraviolet) to dry, unless metallic "driers" are added.

On the other hand, depending on the kind and amount of coloring added, some oil varnishes dry too fast for easy brushing. One can thin the varnish and improve brushing by adding **spirits of gum turpentine**, but **oil of rosemary or lavender** is preferable. Always add a little at a time and test before brushing onto the violin.

COLORED VARNISH — Either **oil** or **spirit varnish** can be *clear* or *colored*. **Clear** varnish is used as an undercoat or sealer or as a topcoat. It usually has an "amber" appearance, but is in effect colorless.

Colored varnish contains *dyes* or fine "transparent" *pigments*, and is applied of course between the clear or yellow undercoat and the clear outer coat(s). Ordinary colored varnish makes up the bulk of the applied varnish, the color intensifying with each coat. But in the case of a **"glaze"** the color is applied in a very thin concentrated layer or layers. (We are not using a glaze here.)

Transparent, relatively permanent color of any hue or intensity can easily be given to *spirit varnish* with good *lightfast* aniline dyes.

Oil varnishes, however, are generally more difficult to color deeply and permanently. Many new makers have been shocked to see much of the color fade out of their varnish as it dried. This depends on the lightfastness of the colorant, the chemistry of the varnish and environmental and other factors.

There are no completely stable colors. Get the colored varnish, or the clear varnish with compatible "lightfast" colorants from a long established reputable supplier, follow their instructions, and test on scrap wood for at least a day in the sun before putting it on your violin. You may be amazed at how much some commercial violin varnishes (even from reputable suppliers) fade.

"Liquid extracts" such as I am using here, are often aniline dyes. In general, pigments are more permanent, but may also fade in oil varnish. It may be not so much a question of lightfastness as the acidity of the varnish.

[Some specially prepared oil varnishes have more or less intense and permanent **color "built-in"** as part of the cooking or other chemical process.

Some makers like to control every part of their process and produce their own coloring material from natural sources. This typically involves the extraction of a **lake pigment** from vegetable material, for example, madder root. This (or commercially available pigments) is then finely ground into a little oil with a muller on ground glass and used to color the clear varnish. Such recipes are outside the scope of this book.]

Having said all this by way of introduction, I will now proceed to varnish my violin, describing the steps only as a demonstration or *example of one way to varnish.* (I have never varnished exactly the same way twice.)

THE GROUND — Before we can apply the varnish proper we have to prepare the **"ground"** for it. We will do this in two steps, *color adjustment* (if any), and *sealing* ("sizing").

[These steps could be done in either order, and separate or combined. Many other materials and methods could be selected.

A common method begins with a "sizing" of 5% **gelatin** solution, which is similar to the traditional glue ground. Doubtless it works well, preventing the uneven absorption of stain, but I prefer not to use it on principle, as hygroscopic and water soluble.

An alcohol solution of **gamboge** gum (poison), which colors yellow and seals at the same time has often been used.

Linseed oil rubbed *into* the wood and let dry and tan in the sun for a long time is also a traditional ground, which may penetrate deeply and harden over time.

Potassium bichromate (poison) is a traditional ground stain, but if you use it, use it sparingly. It is a bright yellow orange solution that reacts in light with the wood to tan it. This is a "neck stain" often used in resurfacing necks. Used excessively as a body stain, it can eventually result in blotchy greenish undertones.

Potassium permanganate is another overused "stain" that is best avoided in favor of a true water stain. It is a bright purple in fresh solution, which quickly oxidizes and leaves a brown residue on the wood that can become ugly.

If you have lots of time you could hang the white untreated violin in the **sun** to tan (oxidize) before varnishing. But it's hard to keep it clean without a sealer. Some use **ozone** to do this fast.]

PRELIMINARY COLOR ADJUSTMENT —

Note: *Never apply any **strong stain** to the bare wood.* It would penetrate much more deeply into the end grain areas, causing a "blotchy" look. It would also make the light wood between the reeds darker than the reeds, causing an unnatural "negative" appearance.

However, a *very **light** water stain* may be used to equalize the wood color (if the spruce is, for example, whiter than the maple), or to accentuate the grain of the maple, or to set a basic color undertone. *Be careful; while this step is not essential, it can be a bad mistake if overdone.*

My Oregon maple is a light reddish tan, and would not really need an added ground color. The Engelmann spruce front, however, is a little lighter, and I would like to match it to the maple color, otherwise the yellow first oat of varnish will look *very* yellow. We could make up and sponge on a *very dilute* aniline water stain of the wanted color, wiping off any excess with a paper towel. We want a consistent color that gives a "head start" to the varnish color, and enhances rather than obscures the grain of the wood. It also prevents white wood from showing when the varnish is chipped. This ground color should be lighter than, and different in hue to the upper color coats. This will give help give a "dichroic" effect, in which the apparent varnish color changes with angle and light.

In this case I used an amber (actually a slightly reddish orange) **natural water stain** from the European suppliers of the oil varnish used below. I applied this (after diluting and testing on scrap spruce) to the whole violin. It raised the grain again somewhat, so after it was dry I once again rubbed off the "wood whiskers." This color may look a little strange to you, but it will change, so be of good faith.

A NOTE ON THE NECK — Of course we do not "varnish" the neck. There should be no sharp boundary between the varnish and neck finish; these should blend into one another. We can do this earlier by feathering the varnish with brush or finger, or later if necessary with a scraper or fine sandpaper.

In the case of this violin, I had already finished the final shaping of the neck, and decided to lightly *stain* and *seal* it *now* for safe handling, but of course leaving the linseed oil and French polish until after replacing the fingerboard.

The *more usual way* is to wait until later for reinstalling the fingerboard, sanding, raising the grain with water, sanding, staining with "neck stain" (such as potassium bichromate solution), filling with linseed oil, and

French polishing. The linseed oil may be applied two or three times and rubbed if necessary. Artist's linseed oil contains a drier, and it is not even necessary for it to be completely dry before **French polishing**, which is the normal neck maintenance procedure. See *Violin Maker's Notebook*, page 37.

SEALING THE WOOD — The **sealing** (or sizing or filling) has been done successfully with all sorts of stuff from acacia gum to egg whites. Its purpose is to prevent the oil varnish from penetrating into the wood. We will simply use a thin **spirit varnish**. The idea is to apply it sparingly so it quickly dries, sealing the wood surface without itself penetrating excessively. It can be applied with brush or cloth, and the excess wiped off promptly. It should not build up on the surface. If it does, wipe off the excess with alcohol on a cloth. Reapply if necessary. Rub this smooth after drying completely.

[Sealing is most important on the porous spruce soundboard, and some apply it only there. However the maple I use is also very absorbent, and I seal it to keep out the oil varnish. I don't want to debate the good or bad acoustic effects of impregnating the wood with various sealers (inside or out). But this seems to work well and look good.]

After rubbing, and before applying a coat of varnish, always vacuum off the dust or at least wipe clean with a damp paper towel and let dry.

THE VARNISH PROPER

I am using an ordinary **violin oil varnish** (*"Öllack"*) from Germany. It dries *more or less* within 24 hours, depending on the temperature and thickness, and is more durable and convenient than varnishes with propolis or other gums that stay soft.

[This varnish may accept and retain color better, and remain softer than the clear varnish I mentioned on page 32 of *Violin Maker's Notebook*. At least it is intended to, while the other varnish is not, although it may work.]

The *liquid* **coloring "extracts"** made for the purpose are used to adjust the color according to your preference. Use *enough* coloring to offset some *inevitable* degree of fading, and to avoid having to use too much varnish to get the required color.

But don't use more than about 10% of typical extracts. And be sure the varnish brushes and levels well, or you may have a real mess with a dark color. I made the color very dark to use fewer coats, but this is harder to handle.

LIQUID MEASURES — It is more convenient to use the prepared liquid varnish, solvents, and liquid extracts than to weigh, dissolve, etc. dry materials.

These are generally packaged in Europe in ml or cc. The US maker may want to use smaller, disposable containers, so I have described here a simple way to make repeatable color concentrations in small quantity — as for one violin.

For example use one **fluid ounce** (oz.) wide mouth **glass jars** with screw top lids. (The kind Christmas jellies come in.) Fill one with colorless varnish. Add the color extract in **drops** either from a dropper bottle or with an **eye dropper**. This is not very accurate, but sufficient for the purpose, if we use the same dropper each time. By recording the number of drops of each color added, the hue and intensity can be reproduced or changed as required.

For reference, the following table *approximately* relates **US *fluid* measures** to **international metric** ml (or cc):

1 dram ≈ 3.7 ml
1 ounce ≈ 30 ml
1 pint ≈ 473 ml

For example, 70 drops into 1 fluid ounce, in my case, was *about* a 5% solution. (A *minim* is 1/60 *dram* and is called a "drop" but differs from our real drops.)

Of course if you are working with larger quantities, use larger metric containers and a graduated cylinder calibrated in ml for the extracts.

SOME VARNISHING RULES:

1 — Always **test** varnish first on similar scrap woods or finishes for brushing, leveling, drying, color, lightfastness, rubbing qualities, etc. before using it on your violin.

2 — Don't brush directly from the varnish container. Pour a small amount into a small **paper cup**. Discard the cup and contents afterwards; don't reuse it.

3 — If there is any sediment or thickening in the varnish, **filter** it through a small piece of linen handkerchief or nylon stocking as you pour it into the cup.

4 — Use high quality **brushes**. Red sable are the best but *expensive*. **25 mm (1 in)** and up to 40 mm (1.5 in) widths are usable. The smaller, especially with oil varnish, is adequate for the whole violin. Experts may want larger brushes for speed, especially with spirit varnish.

Treat them with care. Never try to bend one that has even partially hardened. First soften and clean it in an appropriate solvent or "brush cleaner."

After use, squeeze out the varnish into a paper towel. Then rinse the brush in fresh spirits of gum turpentine in another paper cup. Repeat with ethyl alcohol or acetone. Discard the used solvents. Then wash with warm — not hot — running water and a little mild liquid soap. Rinse well with warm water. Dry with a paper towel, shape, wrap it in a clean paper towel and put it away horizontally in the brush drawer.

[If you are using the brush every day, you can store it in a closed glass jar partly full of solvent — spirits of gum turpentine for oil varnish. The brush should not touch the bottom, but hang from a hook attached to the lid. Gently squeeze out the excess varnish from the brush with a paper towel before placing in the jar, and likewise the excess solvent when removing it. See the photo on page 71.]

5 — Let each coat **dry** thoroughly, **rub** it, and remove any **dust** before the next coat is applied. (See RUBBING below)

6 — Varnish in **daylight** so the true colors can be seen, but not in bright sun so it doesn't dry too fast.

7 — If something goes badly wrong and the varnish has to be **removed**, use ethyl alcohol for spirit varnish, or spirits of gum turpentine for oil varnish. Try to remove the color varnish first, so it does not get into the wood. This will be easy in the case of oil varnish if the under coat(s) have already dried hard. They can then be removed if necessary with paint remover. (This has probably happened to all of us at one time, but let's not dwell on it.)

8 — Be aware of the complexity of color and light. *A varnished violin may look brown in the shade, greenish under fluorescent lighting, red under incandescent, and golden in the sun!*

THE FIRST COLOR VARNISH COAT — The **first coat** is *yellow* to give a golden undertone and further seal the wood against any uneven color penetration of the darker coats to follow. The orange color of the water stain has now given place to a beautiful amber. Rub this smooth when dry and apply one more coat of yellow.

The number of coats needed depends on how thin your varnish is and how thinly you brush it out. Thin is better than thick. Oil varnish is flowed on with a wet brush over an area, then brushed back and forth crosswise to level. Pick up any excess varnish with the brush and park it in an unvarnished area or press it out against the side of the varnish cup.

Smooth the varnish before it gets tacky with light lengthwise sweeping strokes. Brush *toward* the corners of the ribs and the soundholes to avoid leaving varnish pools or runs. With a nearly empty brush remove excess varnish from edges and wherever it threatens to *sag*.

RUBBING — Every coat of varnish should be **"rubbed"** after drying. This knocks off minor bumps and "scuffs" the shine, improving the adhesion of the next coat. We need a *resilient* material for rubbing that conforms to the curves of the violin, and preferably also to the raised grain lines of the front. We do *not* want a rigid sanding block. The finer grades of a **synthetic mesh material** available at hardware stores work well. I prefer it to splintery, rusty **steel wool**. We do not want to actually remove much of the varnish, which would defeat our purpose.

Before any rubbing the varnish must be *sufficiently* hard. Be careful not to rub *through* the coat, especially on crisp edges or raised front grain. Rub *in* the channel, but not *on* the crest of the edge. On the spruce front of the violin, rub the first coats lightly and with the grain to avoid losing the "corduroy" texture. But on the later color coats we can rub across the grain to reduce the ridges, while leaving the varnish in the valleys.

[You could also rub between the coats with tripoli or pumice with water, or the commercial diatomaceous earth **rubbing compound** mentioned below and in *Violin Makers Notebook* on page 37. Such materials are applied on a piece of 6 mm thick **felt** just wide enough to fit the ribs. Care is needed because they are opaque and hide the work. Wipe and check progress frequently. Of course they must be completely removed before varnishing again.]

Careful *wet* sanding with 600 grit paper on a soft rectangular block pencil eraser is also a way of leveling bumps or minor lap marks, especially on the sides and back. But this should not be done until the varnish is sufficiently thick, and preferably only on the final clear coat. Wipe frequently with a paper towel to check progress. Use a light motion following the curvature of the rib surface, *not flat*. Sanding color varnish can make the color uneven. *Be very careful not to rub through!*

THE MAIN COLOR COATS — The next coats, about three or four in the present instance, are of the **main color varnish**. I am using a dark brown, as I want to get sufficient color but keep the varnish fairly thin, which is always desirable. We also want to avoid a garish color. Watch out for the red; it likes to take over. But some red and yellow can add warmth and interest. Different colors may fade differently during drying, so first *test*. You can change the color of successive coats for the effect you like as the color builds. Some coloring materials *accelerate* drying; they act like metallic dryers, containing, for example, iron or manganese, e.g. umber. Others may *retard* drying.

[A **glaze** varnish was mentioned above. This is not part of the method described here. Its commendable purpose is to get a lot of color without a lot of varnish. A glaze basically consists of artist's oil paint applied in a very thin, semi-transparent layer over a smoothly rubbed and polished under-varnish. It is brushed or wiped on, then mostly wiped off, leaving only a little color, which is then smoothed or shaded with fingers, cloth, or special brush techniques. This is then varnished over with a transparent or colorless coat. It may result in a more or less muddy or opaque look, depending on the pigment and the skill of the glazer. Pigments used are the fairly transparent ones such as burnt sienna, brown madder, and burnt umber. It is often convenient in repair work, and can be used as a quick fix, if you happen to rub through the color on the edge of your new violin.]

A limited glaze layer could also be used along with our varnish process here, whether to supplement the color in the varnish, to add another color tone, or to put a little restrained darker shading in the recesses of the edge overhang or scroll — if that is to your taste.]

THE CLEAR TOP COAT — After the last color coat we will apply an outer coat of clear varnish. A special varnish called *Überzugslack* in German may be used. Don't use more coats of this than necessary. It only adds bulk, not color. Its purpose is to allow rubbing *smooth* without affecting color and provide a durable overcoat. Test to see that it brushes and levels well, and is not too thick. If necessary add a little oil of lavender or of rosemary.

[I sometimes skip it altogether, *carefully* polishing the last color coat, but I can't recommend that with this process.]

POLISHING

When the "overcoat" varnish has sufficiently hardened — several days or several weeks — depending on the varnish and its environment, it is rubbed and polished prior to refitting up. I use the commercial paste **rubbing compound** referred to above on a felt pad.

[You may use instead fine **pumice** or **tripoli** with water, followed by **rottenstone** or **Vienna chalk (Wienerkalk)** with light, acid-free, mineral rubbing oil — or water — on a new felt pad. I dislike rubbing with oil; with water you can clean up easily with a damp paper towel. But use what works best with your varnish.]

The final step is a brisk rub with one of the commercial violin "creme" cleaner-polishes on a cloth. These usually have a milky white appearance and contain a very mild "cleaner" or solvent, wax, and a little very mild polishing powder in suspension.

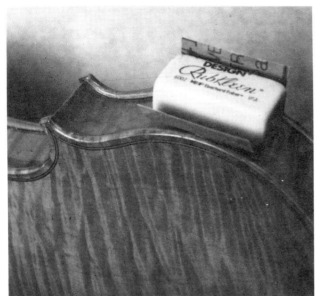

A SOFT "SANDING BLOCK": CAUTION!

POLISHING AFTER RUBBING

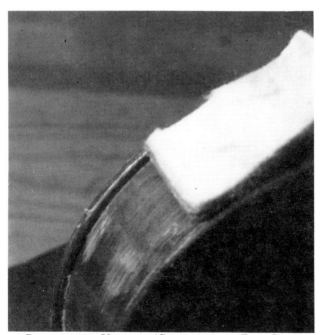

RUBBING THE VARNISH (COMPOUND ON FELT PAD)

[Depending on the varnish, one might also finish up with French polish. *See Violin Maker's Notebook*, pages 36-37.]

Touch up anything that needs it. The **inside of the pegbox** and the **inner edges of the soundholes** can of course be left merely varnished. (Avoid any thick buildup there.) But my preference is to paint these *burnt umber*. It looks elegant, better than black. Thin some burnt umber from a tube of artist's oil paint with a little turpentine spirits to an opaque paint and apply with a small artist's brush. Don't worry if you get some on the finished varnished surface; it easily wipes off with a paper towel over your finger. Let this dry thoroughly before fitting up.

SUMMARY OF VARNISHING STEPS

The foregoing description of the process of varnishing used on my demonstration violin is wordy, and perhaps confusing with the mention of various alternatives.

Let's *review* this process **"step by step"** as I did it. This is *only one way* of many. It is, however, a standard, straightforward (if slow) method.

I have made an exception here to my rule of not mentioning **brand names** in this book. This is done as a *working example* only, not necessarily a product endorsement, and certainly not a guarantee. The varnish materials mentioned below are available from several major European and US violin supply companies.

(See SOURCES AND SUPPLIERS on page 8 of this book. Also see page 38 of *Violin Maker's Notebook*.)

[Many fine varnish materials are available, but be aware that formulations and quality of some can vary from time to time, especially those repackaged for sale under house names.]

1 — Moisten the instrument with a wet **sponge**. Let it dry completely.

2 — Rub smooth with a synthetic mesh **wood finishing pad**, for example, *3M no. 7415*. (Finer grades are preferable for rubbing the varnish in the rubbing steps below. Rub very carefully and lightly or it may leave deep scratches. Work with the adjustable bench light to monitor the progress, and always remove the dust before varnishing!)

3 — Dilute the **ground stain (Beize)**, for example, *Hammerl (JOHA) Stain No. 423* (or, in my case, *GEWA 464.004*) with an equal amount of water. Test on a scrap of your spruce including end grain. Apply with a sponge and let dry. (This gives a "salmon" color.) Rub.

4 — Brush on the **spirit ground varnish (Grundlack)**, e.g. *Hammerl*, quickly and evenly. (I diluted *Behlen's Violin Varnish* with an equal amount of ethyl alcohol.)

5 — Within a few minutes wipe off any excess spirit varnish from the surface with a **cloth** wet with alcohol. (We want to *seal*, not *coat* the surface.) Let dry completely. Rub smooth.

6 — Use a good colorless **Violin Oil Varnish (Öllack)**, *e.g Hammerl*, with *sufficient* **liquid golden yellow extract for oil varnish (Farbextrakt für Öllack)**. I used about 5% (70 drops in 1 fluid ounce). Brush on a *thin, level* coat. (I did not find it necessary to thin this with spirits of gum turpentine.) Dry completely. (At least overnight in warm weather.) Rub. Repeat once.

7 — Repeat step 6 but with the main color **"brown" varnish** as needed for desired coverage and color. I used 90 drops of **brown extract,** e.g. *Hammerl (*I used *GEWA 464.157)* and 30 of **red extract**. The optional red was to warm up the brown. The varnish was tacky and difficult to brush. (Coloring may do this.) This was easily corrected by the addition of just enough — 10% or so of **oil of rosemary** — I don't remember exactly how much, but I did *test* first on a scrap fiddle, as you should. It was quite dark for an oil varnish, and I used only three coats. Each coat lightens as it dries, finishing with the desired color. (Note: The manufacturer recommends only 5 % extract but more, thinner coats for the desired color, which makes the brushing easier.)

8 — Brush on **Oil Finishing Varnish with Lavender (Überzugslack)**, e.g. *Hammerl*. This takes longer to dry (several days). Rub. Repeat. Let dry *hard*. (At least a week in *warm* weather.)

9 — If necessary remove any "specks" or bumps with **600 wet sandpaper**. "Rub and polish" with **Meguiar's No. 4** on a 6 mm thick **felt pad**. Remove with a paper

towel. Polish with a good **"creme" violin polish** on a cloth.

[The process is similar with spirit varnish except for different application techniques — spraying or more difficult brushing and leveling. And it is easier to get deeper, permanent color with spirit varnishes.]

FINAL FITTINGS

This is really a misnomer, since our final fittings are of course only the first of many for our violin. But now we want to dress it in its "presentation" fittings — *simple, elegant, functional.*

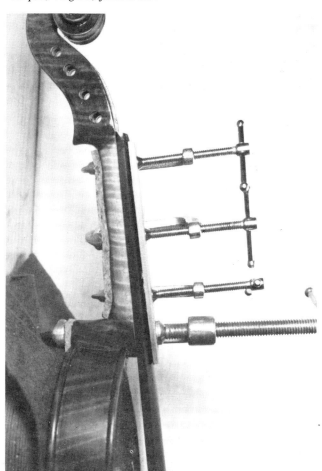

GLUING ON THE FINGERBOARD

Glue the **fingerboard** precisely back into its original place. We are not using alignment pins, but it's easy if the glue is not too thick and we have made a central groove in the back of the fingerboard. Use padded clamps, and test by feeling with the finger tips that the edges are perfectly lined up. We don't want to narrow the neck with any unnecessary rescraping because of a poor gluing job.

The photo shows one of several good clamping arrangements. I use a **softwood strip** on top and **6 mm thick cork pads** underneath.

[Special plastic fingerboard clamps are available, if you prefer.]

The **peg holes** need to be cleaned of any varnish with a touch of the reamer, the **pegs** refitted if necessary, and peg compound applied. Change the **bridge** or even make a new one if you like. Check the **tail gut** length, the **end button** fitting, **E - tuner**, and nut and bridge string **grooves**. Readjust the **soundpost**, or fit another if appropriate, but don't fret about it.

SOME RETROSPECTIVE NOTES ON FINISHING — The SURFACE PREPARATION process on page 71 suggests not sanding before wetting, and not sanding or rescraping after wetting to raise the grain, before varnishing. It was explained that this was intended to give a more "hand carved" look. However, this is not to everyone's taste, and may, depending on the wood texture and the maker's skill in scraping, result in an excessively rough or wavy surface. You may prefer to sand and/or scrape smooth and wet, let dry, then resand or rescrape before beginning the process, especially on the maple, where a smoother surface is usually expected. (Or even perhaps skip the water altogether if you do not use a water based ground stain.) This is a matter of personal taste and technique.

I continue to use the same VARNISH PROPER materials and process as described beginning of page 73. This has been very satisfactory to me, but as I have pointed out, coloring *oil* varnish is problematical and often subject to some degree of early fading, depending on the exact materials used. If this is a problem for you, consider using a pigmented glaze (although less transparent), or a good spirit varnish colored with "lightfast" aniline dyes.

AFTERWORD

Enjoy the fruit of your labors. Play your violin, then sell it and make another for yourself — until someone has to have it. (Happily mine was sold as I began it, which helped underwrite the cost of this book.)

As usual, I worried over graduating and varnishing. I am pleased now. The varnish refined the tone and finished a rich warm brown. This violin is powerful, fast, sonorous. May yours be even better!

HAS